perspectives
ON DESIGN

design philosophies expressed by florida's leading professionals

Published by

PANACHE
PANACHE PARTNERS, LLC

13747 Montfort Drive, Suite 100
Dallas, Texas 75240
972.661.9884
Fax: 972.661.2743
www.panache.com

Publishers: Brian G. Carabet and John A. Shand
Executive Publisher: Phil Reavis
Group Publisher: Sheri Lazenby
Director of Development & Design: Beth Benton
Editor: Elizabeth Gionta
Designer: Emily A. Kattan

Printed in Malaysia

Distributed by Independent Publishers Group
800.888.4741

PUBLISHER'S DATA

Perspectives on Design Florida

Library of Congress Control Number: 2007920300

ISBN 13: 978-1-933415-37-6
ISBN 10: 1-933415-37-1

First Printing 2007

10 9 8 7 6 5 4 3 2 1

Previous Page: Mystic Granite & Marble, *Page 101*

This Page: Summer Classics, *Page 283*

perspectives
ON DESIGN

design philosophies expressed by florida's leading professionals

Above: Gallery 17·92, *Page 229*
Facing Page Left: O'Guin Decorative Arts, LLC, *Page 245*
Facing Page Right: Hall Bell Aqüi, Inc., *Page 253*

introduction

Creating the spaces in which we live and achieving the beauty we desire can be a daunting quest—a quest that is as diverse as each of our unique personalities. For some, it may be a serene, infinity-edge saltwater pool in the backyard, for others it may be an opulent marble entryway with bronze insets imported from Italy. Aspiring chefs may find a kitchen boasting the finest in technology their true sanctuary.

Perspectives on Design Florida is a pictorial journey from conceptualizing your dream home to putting together the finishing touches, to creating an outdoor oasis. Alongside the phenomenal photography, you will have a rare insight to how these tastemakers achieve such works of art and be inspired by their personal perspectives on design.

Within these pages, the state's finest artisans will share their wisdom, experience and talent. It is the collaboration between these visionaries and the outstanding pride and craftsmanship of the products showcased that together achieve the remarkable. Learn from leaders in the industry about the aesthetics of a finely crafted sofa, how appropriate lighting can dramatically change the appearance of a room, or what is necessary to create a state-of-the-art home theater.

Whether your dream is to have a new home or one that has been redesigned to suit your lifestyle, *Perspectives on Design Florida* will be both an enjoyable journey and a source of motivation.

chapter one: the concept

erickson associates 17

jonathan parks architect 25

randall stofft architects 33

richard skinner & associates, p.l. architects 41

savoie architects, p.a. 49

chapter two: the structure

davis dunn construction, inc. 59

the hill group. 67

morales construction company, inc. .75

newbury north associates 83

pellegrini homes 91

chapter three: elements of structure

mystic granite & marble 101

tischler und sohn. 111

architectural artworks incorporated. 121

island tile & stone, inc.. 127

olde world cabinetry. 133

safe: strategically armored & fortified environments 139

wonderland products 145

amazon metal fabricators 151

get organized, inc.. 155

hyland custom cabinetry. 159

klahm & sons. 163

moyer marble & tile company 167

preston studios 171

Left: Rick Moore, *Page 249*

table of contents

chapter four: elements of design

beasley & henley interior design 175

advanced audio design 183

clive christian home 195

geary design 205

thomas riley artisans' guild 211

artisan inc. 217

c.w. smith imported antiques 221

feature presentation 225

gallery 17·92 229

gulf south kitchen design 233

michael schmidt custom interiors 237

murano glass creations 241

o'guin decorative arts, llc 245

rick moore fine art gallery 249

chapter five: living the elements

hall bell aqüí, inc. 253

the hughes group 261

tropical pools & spas 269

florida water gardens 277

summer classics 283

summer classics at fireplace & verandah 289

outdoor lighting perspectives® 293

tc water features, inc. 297

"By wisdom a house is built, and through understanding, it is established; through knowledge its rooms are filled with rare and beautiful treasures."

~Proverb

Tropical Pools & Spas, *Page 269*

Pellegrini Homes, *Page 91*

Jonathan Parks Architect, *Page 25*

TC Water Features, Inc., *Page 297*

Mystic Granite & Marble, *Page 101*

Davis Dunn Construction, Inc., *Page 59*

The Hill Group, *Page 67*

Richard Skinner & Associates, *Page 41*

"There is nothing that makes its way more directly to the soul than beauty."

~Joseph Addison

Left: Tropical Pools & Spas, *Page 269*

"We exist only to discover beauty; all else is a form of waiting."

~Kahlil Gibran

First: Olde World Cabinetry, *Page 133*
Second: Randall Stofft Architects, *Page 33*
Third: Olde World Cabinetry, *Page 133*
Fourth: Geary Design, *Page 205*
Facing Page: Klahm & Sons, *Page 163*

Erickson Associates, *Page 17*   Jonathan Parks Architect, *Page 25*

the concept

chapter one

Randall Stofft Architects, *Page 33*

Richard Skinner & Associates, *Page 41*

Savoie Architects, P.A., *Page 49*

Before he even knew the word "architect," Carl Erickson knew he wanted to be one. The built environment always fascinated him and coupled with his penchant towards drawing interesting structures, his intrigue with design grew. After five very busy years in his Connecticut practice, Carl decided to relocate the firm to Naples. It proved to be a wise decision; within two months the firm had secured two of the most significant residential commissions in all of Collier County.

Today, Erickson Associates is a mid-size residential/commercial firm, which focuses on designing "homes of significance" and all that this mantra implies. A home of significance is achieved when the needs and qualities homeowners desire in their future residences are taken to the highest level and centrally focused on a common language throughout. The firm handles the design of all cabinetry, trimwork, hardscapes, and garden and water features to cohesively achieve this principle. Erickson and Associates' work spans the nation with current and completed projects in Montana, Connecticut, Texas, Michigan, Minnesota, Wisconsin and Pennsylvania as well as Florida.

"The many facets of contrast are a most useful tool in successful architectural composition."

~Carl Erickson

ERICKSON ASSOCIATES

"These are classic examples of how the owner that is willing to take risks always ends up with the best result."

~Carl Erickson

This was designed for a client who desired a high level of privacy but still wanted to create a stunning façade which would also elevate the context of the neighborhood, always a consideration. There are minimal windows on the first floor though we are able to take attention away from that fact by playing up positive and negative space with the sun's cast as well as thoughtful landscaping *(Previous Pages)*.
Photograph by Kim Sargent

The back of the home dissolves into an antithesis of the front façade—yet still maintains design integrity—with expansive windows that showcase a beautiful view of a beach with the Indian River and ocean beyond *(Above & Facing Page)*.
Photography by Kim Sargent

One of the first large-scaled homes in an evolving neighborhood, this residence uses a careful play of positive and negative space, scale and articulation to deliver the formality and detail the owner desired while remaining sympathetic to its site and community *(Facing Page Top)*.
Photograph by Erickson Associates

While located in a beachfront high-rise where the typical stylistic language was a formalized "Mediterranean," we instead played with the imagery and character of a beachfront cottage. The result is a relaxed and friendly residence with astounding views of the local estuaries and gulf *(Facing Page Bottom)*.
Photograph by Doug Thompson Photography, Inc.

Use of reclaimed old-growth yellow pine beams from the original structure—this type of wood is impossible to find new—was a risk that paid off. Additionally, the fireplace is a found object and the cabinets are made from old-growth pecky cypress that was also reclaimed from the original structure. The result is a delighted client who now enjoys a space made completely original *(Above)*.
Photograph by Bruce Starrenburg ©www.BStarrenburg.com

"Choose identifying attributes that will allow the space to stand out with pride and fascination."

~Carl Erickson

The focus of this room had to, of course, be the view of the mountains. This remote home is full of elements of magic and comfort. There was to be a story around every corner *(Above Left).*
Photograph by Kim Sargent

Within the same home we designed a children's room inspired by the children's book *Where The Wild Things Are (Above Right).*
Photograph by Kim Sargent

We designed this grand entry hall to offer a sequential introduction to the rewards of view, water, beach, lawns, terraces and rooms. The shape of the space, the materials used on the floors and walls, the nature of the lighting; all are used to lead the eye along the main axis of the home, which in this case terminates with the master suite. Sequence is an essential quality in any home of significance *(Facing Page).*
Photograph by Bruce Starrenburg

As principal of one of Florida's fastest growing architecture firms, Jonathan Parks credits their success to great clients and a skilled, uncompromising team dedicated to the same ideal, "that architecture can change the way we live."

From new construction to historical restoration, from luxury residences to large-scale commercial projects, the experts of Jonathan Parks Architect appreciate the diversity of client projects in which they are involved because no two designs are ever the same. JPA designs by the philosophy that individuality is priceless.

With sameness overrunning communities across the country—in all spheres, from residential to commercial—the truly special places will be the unique spaces that have been carefully and originally designed. The architects and designers of JPA believe that designing timeless architecture from the inside out is the best way to ensure that each layout is truly a portrait of how the client wants to live.

"Working with clients is one of the best parts of being an architect;
I relish the exchange of ideas and collaboration with them."

~Jonathan Parks

JONATHAN PARKS ARCHITECT

"Our work blurs the boundaries between interior and exterior spaces."

~Jonathan Parks

The redesign of the interior of this home stripped it to its basic elements, removed many walls and raised a portion of the roof to add space within the same footprint. The renovation added deck surfaces, open spaces for entertaining, and introduced the kitchen as the focal point. The bayou and pool were connected to the home through the use of sliding, pocketing doors and wider terraces. This remodel captures the elegance of its owners and delivers a home that is functional, open and unembellished *(Above)*.
Photograph by The Greg Wilson Group

With the intent to downsize from their previous residence, the owners purchased this modest home within an established community on the Gulf of Mexico. The original 1970s' design featured a three-story home wrapped in outdated horizontal siding and a warren of small dark rooms. They teamed with the architect for a thorough redesign that would reflect their taste of clean, simple lines filled with open space *(Above)*.
Photograph by The Greg Wilson Group

Situated on two-plus acres, this 3,200-square-foot Sarasota residence, designed for a young, active family, reflects the desire for a minimalist home in which they could equally live and entertain. The concept of the layout was to create a separation of these functions with architectural elements, yet tie the design together with light, form and repetition. Using non-traditional building materials the owners' request for an energy-efficient home was achieved *(Previous Pages)*.
Photograph by Tom Jefferds

Inside the 625-square-foot hurricane-safe pool house, eight-foot-high glass doors disappear into the walls, opening the structure to the pool and courtyard. Traditional Japanese shoji screens, glass block, exposed ventilation and indirect lighting merge to create an inviting space with an artistic edge *(Above)*.
Photograph by The Greg Wilson Group

A freestanding addition to an existing historically designated Florida home, this project was designed to create an outdoor living environment. The homeowners, both design professionals, requested a pool house, pool and landscape layout that embraced a modern design and blurred the boundaries between indoor and outdoor spaces while meeting historic home guidelines—all within a compact urban backyard. The result is a serene indoor/outdoor area exemplifying how architectural design can change the way people live *(Facing Page)*.
Photograph by The Greg Wilson Group

Located on a barrier island in the Gulf of Mexico, this 5,500-square-foot vacation home was designed to reflect the homeowners' desire to relax and spend time with family. The concept of the layout was to maximize waterfront views and prevailing off-shore breezes. The uncluttered design, palette of simple finishes, wealth of windows and high ceilings create a sense of interior and exterior space that is wide open without ignoring privacy. The kitchen, where the homeowner spends a great deal of time, was carefully designed to extend out of the home with wide open windows and a view of water on three sides. Each level features balconies or a patio for outdoor enjoyment and relaxation *(Above)*.
Photograph by The Greg Wilson Group

"Great architecture does not have to be expensive."

~Jonathan Parks

The method of design at Jonathan Parks Architect focuses on purpose and balance *(Top, Center & Bottom)*.
Top & Bottom Photography by Camille Pyatte; Center Photograph by The Greg Wilson Group

With a picturesque location on the Gulf of Mexico, the challenge of this project was to achieve a design that would accommodate the owner's relaxed lifestyle. In order to successfully accomplish these goals, the design focused on maximizing detail, light and flow. The layout of the floor plan incorporates views of the water while organic patterns merge with clean symmetry for a sleek, yet inviting atmosphere. The primary feature became the curve of the roofline, raised to 16 feet, which was designed to simulate the lines of a yacht *(Facing Page)*.
Photograph by The Greg Wilson Group

Randall Stofft describes his style as "Classical Tropical," noting that all details are based on classical proportions and lines. His scope of work reaches well beyond that genre to reveal influences from the most emulated, diverse styles throughout history. These styles include Palladian, Mediterranean, Craftsman, Modern and what he has termed "Old Florida Revisionist," a return to the old tin-roofed colonial outpost look most popular in the islands decades ago. Randall Stofft Architects enjoys the range of projects they are entrusted with, from smaller "jewel box" homes to substantial estate residences, including notable and unique projects such as a palatial 60,000-square-foot residence in Manalapan, Florida. His portfolio equally encompasses commercial and resort design, with Randall at the helm to ensure that each project is as extraordinary as it is original—an individualized celebration of the architectural design experience. Randall Stofft's respect of region blended with international and global influences has become the hallmark of the man and his architectural firm that today, with his West Coast partner John Cooney, consists of 50 employees and five offices in Delray Beach, Vero Beach and Naples, Florida; the Caribbean and Cleveland, Ohio.

"It is balance——not symmetry——that results in timeless, interesting architecture."

~Randall Stofft

RANDALL STOFFT ARCHITECTS

"A Florida home must be sculpted from the exterior views and spaces."

~Randall Stofft

Desiring a much-needed Florida retreat, a "Wall Streeter" and his wife came to me with the express wishes that their home be both soothing and designed in the Florida vernacular. Created to sit comfortably overlooking the Gulf Dune in Captiva, this inventive home celebrates its regional location while achieving the dreams of its homeowners. We used extensive cantilevered porches and open terraces to create a hovering effect. The design—both inside and out—reflects a laid-back casual elegance that exudes comfort and relaxation. To reinforce this mood from the outside, I chose clapboard siding, shell-infused pavers and statement-making satin-finished metal roofing. Like all of my "influenced designs," this home was not intended to be a replica, only to capture that charm and charisma of some great, early tropical homes. We clearly have moved forward from the massing with our use of light, proportion and volume *(Previous Pages)*.
Photograph by Troy Campbell

Outdoor living is essential in Florida, especially to those with secondary homes who never take these magnificent surroundings for granted. All the comforts of the indoors translate well outdoors with a beautiful ocean view as a spectacular backdrop *(Right)*.
Photograph by Troy Campbell

"Although it is often said, truly, details make a home unique: to the homeowner, to the interpretation of the style and to the landscape."

~Randall Stofft

The storm shutter, although utilitarian, creates an interesting architectural element and is another element that recalls the past *(Facing Page)*.
Photograph by Troy Campbell

An elegant approach to the residence engages the eye toward the dramatic arched entry. Outdoor elements, such as the lush tropical vegetation and fountain are all critical to enhancing the mood of the home *(Above)*.
Photograph by Troy Campbell

A well thought-out pool, as seen from this side view, can accomplish multiple tasks. The fountain encompasses a sculptural element—which creates a lovely, sophisticated effect—as well as infuses the calming sound of cascading water *(Top)*.
Photograph by Troy Campbell

We chose to create special interest with the front entrance, which is the natural primary focus, by creating a low arched entryway and also by allowing the wood door's natural grain to contrast against the light hues of the home *(Center)*.
Photograph by Troy Campbell

As one can better see here, we painted the mahogany windows a sea-foam blue, as well as both the house and shutters gradations of white to reflect our feeling and homage to "Old Florida" *(Bottom)*.
Photograph by Troy Campbell

Another breathtaking rear elevation pool view set against the magnificent ocean, as enjoyed from the outdoor living space *(Facing Page)*.
Photograph by Lori Hamilton

Founded in 1990, Richard Skinner, president of Richard Skinner & Associates, P.L. ARCHITECTS has created an architectural practice employing the most basic principle: listening to the client. He has the innate ability to then transform those dreams into unique, functional and artistic living spaces. Richard's design philosophies are deeply rooted in the traditions of timeless, classic architecture. A house should live well and never be a "monument" to its architect, it should take its cues from the owner and surroundings. His sculptural approach to design includes all aspects of the tangible: views, light, shadow, scale and detail. Each of these qualities is carefully addressed resulting in warm, friendly, and uplifting rooms. Above all, Richard designs all of his homes to convey a sense of delight and timelessness, as if the house could have always been there.

Richard keeps his firm a manageable size as all primary designs originate with him and firm architect David Case. The firm employs the talents of an additional architect and five designers as well as two administrative assistants. Richard Skinner & Associates has been published in numerous magazines, and several projects have received craftsmanship awards as well a design award for merit.

"A house should never be a 'monument' to its architect, but rather should take its cues from its owner and surroundings."

~Richard Skinner

RICHARD SKINNER & ASSOCIATES, P.L. ARCHITECTS

"Every room is an opportunity to create an element of surprise, delight and interest."

~Richard Skinner

 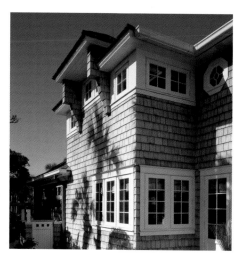 

This cottage-style home was inspired by the client's desire to create wonderful architecture that continued the context of this charming neighborhood within a 1900s' beach community of shingle homes. Every inch of the grounds was addressed in sculpting the entirety of the home. The outdoor spaces were designed to respond to dynamic ocean views on the east side while creating a quiet contemplative courtyard on the west offering protection from northeast gale winds in winter *(Previous Pages)*.

This sitting area nestles up to a small dipping pool that is built into the wood deck. The balcony above offers a breathtaking panoramic view of the ocean and surrounding neighborhood *(Above Left)*.

Within this side wing is the breakfast area. Windows were intentionally placed around the corners to actively engage the surrounding landscape. The octagonal window above adds detail to the outside while discreetly flooding a second-floor bathroom with natural light *(Above)*.

Located at the front of the property, the garage/ guest house and attached pergola create the front "wall" of the courtyard. The pergola serves as a shaded cabana and terminus for the lap pool. The room over the garage offers guests privacy with large windows filling the interior space with natural light *(Above)*.

This outdoor porch engages a quiet courtyard with reflecting pool. Both dining and living rooms share this space making the warm, cozy fireplace outside part of the interior living experience *(Facing Page)*.
Photography by Joe Lapeyra

"In considering all of the structures on the site, we try to step back and look at the neighborhood as a whole. This garage is compatible with the home yet different. It is as if it was added at a different time, similar to the manner in which this historic neighborhood has evolved."

~Richard Skinner

Covered porches are essential in coastal Florida. In addition to extending the living boundaries of the house outside, this porch also protects from sun, rain and gale northeast winds while creating a sheltered connection between front and side decks *(Top)*.

This is the guest house/garage as viewed from the back door of the main house. This building shares elevated views of the courtyard below on one side and engages the active neighborhood foot traffic from the second-floor balcony on the other (not visible here). Wraparound windows give one a sense of all that is going on in the neighborhood *(Bottom)*.

This entry hallway serves as an introduction to the idea that the home is a gallery for art as well as living. Lighting is soft and detailing is minimal yet rich to emphasize the art *(Facing Page)*. *Photography by Joe Lapeyra*

"Every element in a house is a sculptural opportunity that starts with the form and is enhanced with detail."

~Richard Skinner

The kitchen/breakfast room is a reflection of the homeowner's design preferences. The exterior maintains the architectural context of the neighborhood while the interior reflects an austere well-designed modernity *(Above Left)*.

The stair element and the niche beyond reflect how much of the interior of the home was designed; for placement of art or as an art object itself *(Above Right)*.

Like the interior of the house, this lap pool serves as an object of art that anchors the courtyard and reflects the shimmering beauty of the house *(Facing Page)*.
Photography by Joe Lapeyra

Savoie Architects, P.A., holds a great respect for the profession of Architecture and how it can shape a community. The firm is dedicated to providing the client with the best design possible. With the philosophy that the client is an integral part of the design team, they pay particular attention to the client's needs and desires, and how they can shape the design. Savoie Architects is committed to creating a solution that is personal in function and design while respecting the natural beauty of the site and environment.

Matthew C. Savoie is founder and president of Savoie Architects, P.A. and holds a Bachelor of Architecture degree from Louisiana State University in Baton Rouge. He is licensed in the states of Florida, Louisiana and Texas and has been in the architectural field since 1992. As a native of south Louisiana, he was exposed to the richness of architecture that is a large part of Louisiana's heritage.

Andrea J. Plunk is a partner and vice-president in the firm holding a Bachelor of Architecture degree from Auburn University and a Florida license. She has built her career with the full range of Florida's coastal architecture from the formal mansions of Palm Beach County to the casual beach homes of the Panhandle.

"Design has to respond to and revolve around its setting. That's what makes it custom design."

~Matt Savoie

SAVOIE ARCHITECTS, P.A.

The house sits on a bluff and boasts a stunning panoramic view towards the Gulf of Mexico as well as Grayton Beach State Park *(Previous Pages Left & Right)*.
Photography by Andrea J. Plunk

This interior dining area faces both the lake and the gulf. The reality of a coastal location prohibits the physical connection but the visual connection is successfully achieved *(Above)*.
Photograph by Michael Rixon

A picturesque setting on a coastal dune lake provides a beautiful backdrop for a French-influenced coastal Florida home *(Facing Page Left)*.
Photograph by Stephen T. Brinker

This open air dining area faces the lake and the entire house is open to views of the gulf *(Facing Page Right)*.
Photograph by Michael Rixon

"We view design as a culmination of senses and memories in built form."

~Andrea Plunk

"We are both satisfied with our work when good design takes on a physical appearance that both the client and the architect are pleased with."

~Matt Savoie

This interior courtyard, with natural cleft slate flooring, provides a calming atmosphere in which to enjoy a meal with family and friends or a moment of solace *(Facing Page)*.
Photograph by Michael Rixon

Historical components of the "Florida Cracker" vernacular were manipulated to create a design composition that would suit the client's more modern program *(Top)*.
Photograph by Michael Rixon

The interior of the home skillfully interprets its exterior. Using exposed wood detail beams and hardwood flooring as well as a more natural-feeling decor, this interior translates seamlessly to the outdoors. Interior design by Suzanne Harmon, ASID, and Leigh Wright *(Bottom)*.
Photograph by Michael Rixon

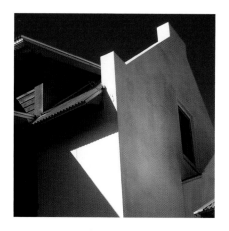

The roof of this primarily stucco house is softened with a cedar-clad dormer *(First)*.
Photograph by Andrea J. Plunk

A mahogany door and custom iron grille *(Second)*.
Photograph by Michael Rixon

This narrow window was incorporated for its more elegant ratio of proportion *(Third)*.
Photograph by Michael Rixon

In using privacy walls/courtyards, focal points are created to be viewed from interior spaces *(Fourth)*.
Photograph by Michael Rixon

To capture the gulf views, this is a three-story home, like many of the beach homes in this part of Florida. Courtyards serve as transitional elements bringing the scale back to the ground plane *(Facing Page)*.
Photograph by Michael Rixon

Davis Dunn Construction, Inc., *Page 59*

The Hill Group, *Page 67*

the structure

chapter two

Morales Construction Company, Inc., *Page 75*

Newbury North Associates, *Page 83*

Pellegrini Homes, *Page 91*

Teaming up in the late 1980s, Whitney Davis and Will Dunn—both Alabama natives and graduates of Auburn University—united their uniquely specialized backgrounds to eventually form Davis Dunn Construction, Inc. in 1991.

Originating from a background in finance, Whit found himself intrigued by the construction sector in which Will worked. Although Will was involved in the commercial side, the two decided to become licensed builders and began their partnership and foray into the industry with modest-sized homes. Through the years and with abundant opportunity in the highly desirable Florida resort town of Destin, the company increased in size and in the expanse of their homes.

Today, with a vision to pare down their projects to focus on a limited number of high-end homes a year, the company prefers to produce superior-quality homes rather than focus on quantity of projects. With breathtaking homes dotting the coastline and town of Destin, Davis Dunn Construction is realizing this ambition with every home. And while countless accolades and industry-wide recognition are not their goals, they continue to be the result.

"As perfectionists, we tirelessly work to elevate the level of our construction. We use only the most dependable and experienced subcontractors, and it shows."

~Whit Davis

DAVIS DUNN CONSTRUCTION, INC.

The challenges with this contemporary oceanfront home were to construct a free-supporting porch as well as blend in the structural necessities while achieving the desired style at the same time. By using commercial-grade concrete construction, we solved any issues and built a very sound home. Integrity of the home is critical, especially in beachfront homes such as this one whose rear exterior faces south to the Gulf of Mexico. Architecture by Christ & Associates Architects and Planners, P.A. *(Previous Pages Left & Right).*
Photography by John Umberger

We built this home on an all-poured structural slab, which means, in the most basic terms, if a hurricane washed the land away, this home would still stand. This gives our clients a great degree of comfort. As you see, the kitchen and living area takes full advantage of its ocean views as a design element. We used reclaimed imported French antique oak on the coffered ceiling, travertine limestone flooring and faux-finished marble-glazed walls. The richness set by the kitchen and ceiling millwork give the ocean view a bit of friendly "competition." Architecture by Prescott Architects; interior design by Kaye Holland Roberts Interior Design *(Right).*
Photograph by Michael Rixon

"Our clients are generally long-distance and we are sensitive to the level of trust they are putting in our hands. We are always available to answer any question, address any type of concern and provide continuous updates on the progress of their projects."

~Will Dunn

Located in Destin Pointe, this West Indies-inspired home offers an unsurpassed southern view of the harbor and Gulf of Mexico at twilight. Built to withstand coastal surges, the residence overlooks 100 yards of dunes. Architecture by Burwell Associates *(Facing Page)*.

Although most of our clients also desire an elevator, as these homes are built to eventually become permanent retirement residences, they also appreciate the artistic beauty of well-crafted stairs. This three-story home offered the chance to showcase the fine craftsmanship of this pyramid-like limestone staircase. The risers are each one large piece of heavy limestone while the stair treads are solid pieces as well. The custom medallion insert and metal railing are framed by a rich mahogany rail cap. Architecture by Prescott Architects; interior design by Kaye Holland Roberts Interior Design *(Above)*.
Photography by Michael Rixon

"We always build as if we are building for ourselves. It's with this personal attachment and solid attention to every detail that we construct all of our homes."

~Whit Davis

"The Retreat." This luxurious master bath features a striking white marble floor and matching freestanding tub. Aside from an amazing view, one's eye is also drawn to the overhanging tongue-and-groove detailing from the roof. Architecture by Thurber Architecture, P.A.; interior design by Fouquet Designs *(Facing Page Top)*.

This was actually begun as a spec home, which found a buyer before construction ended. The home has gulf access and views facing south and west. We constructed this six-bedroom, seven-and-half-bathroom home to maximize space and placed the "hearts of the home," the kitchen and great room, on the second floor to take advantage of the ocean view. Although this was not intended with a specific client in mind, quality was not compromised: The walls and ceiling are comprised entirely of tongue-and-groove wood instead of drywall; there are stone and wood floors throughout, as well as high-grade plantation shutters. Architecture by Savoie Architects, P.A. *(Facing Page Bottom)*.

From this vantage point, one can appreciate the custom turned columns as well as the structure of the railing system found on this Florida-style cottage with Gulf of Mexico views, located in Destin Pointe. This home also boasts a fourth-floor observatory accessed by a spiral staircase. Architecture by Savoie Architects, P.A. *(Right)*. *Photography by Michael Rixon*

Some builders are made. Others were just "born to build." The latter best describes Toby Hill. After earning a degree in construction and working for a large commercial construction firm, he realized that only true custom residential work would expose him to the top creativity by which he was so challenged. In 1984, Toby founded The Hill Group on the tenets of unmatched quality, unrivaled talent and exceptional customer service.

For over two decades, The Hill Group has built some of the most extraordinary high-end residences in the most exclusive areas of South Florida. Toby appreciates that his affluent clientele demand the highest quality craftsmanship and products available and he has made it his mission to unfailingly deliver both.

Unlike any other builder in the region, The Hill Group has a 12,000-square-foot millwork shop along with a 4,000-square-foot fine finishing shop. Both are full of state-of-the-art machinery and uniquely talented craftspeople. They offer well-known architects, designers, and clients from around the country and Europe the opportunity to see their visions expressed as art.

"A homeowner should never compromise on quality design and quality construction; they will both pay huge dividends in the end."

~Toby Hill

THE HILL GROUP

"It is amazing the talent you can draw out of an individual when you provide them with solid leadership, a supportive environment and the proper tools necessary to do what is asked of them."

~Toby Hill

A rear façade view of a residence on Orchid Island at dusk. This magnificent Georgian home was designed by local architect George F. Bollis Jr. Recessed fountains are highlighted by the light beams surrounding the pool area, making a dramatic presentation at night *(Previous Pages)*.
Photograph by George Cott

This Caribbean Colonial-style residence looks out onto the beautiful Intracoastal Waterway. The loggia spans the length of the home, offering differing vantage points and access off various rooms. As the northernmost point in the Tropics, Vero Beach offers the most invigorating blend of Caribbean sunlight and mild, breezy weather *(Right)*.
Photograph by Kim Sargent

"A great builder is distinguished by the experience and breadth of the skilled craftspeople employed. There is no substitute for that."

~Toby Hill

Set amidst manicured grounds, a sculpture garden takes pride of place against the background of this home's magnificent two-story façade *(Above)*.
Photograph by George Cott

This covered lanai enjoys views of the Indian River Lagoon. It also boasts concealed hurricane shutters that can be lowered at the touch of a button *(Facing Page Top)*.
Photograph by George Cott

A handcrafted coffered ceiling lends elegance to this formal dining room. To let the tropical breeze in, French doors are fitted with screens that recess into pockets *(Facing Page Bottom Left)*.
Photograph by George Cott

Exquisite custom millwork, crafted at The Hill Group's dedicated shop, has become the epitome of the firm's quality and attention to detail *(Facing Page Bottom Right)*.
Photograph by George Cott

"Building a truly great custom home is about relationships—challenging relationships that sharpen everyone on the team."

~Toby Hill

 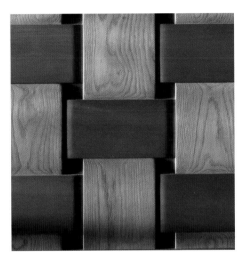 

A hand-crafted operable radius head louver, in American black walnut, was rubbed meticulously with English museum wax to match the entire raised panel study *(Above)*.
Photograph by Rob Downey

This Frank Lloyd Wright-influenced home required some innovation from The Hill Group. Positioned due west to enjoy the beautiful Florida sunsets, shading and screening had to be addressed to make the many openings enjoyable. Their design solution turned out to be not only elegant but hidden and operated by remote control. The dramatic ceiling was designed by architect David Richardson and draws the eye upward to take in the handsome mahogany woodwork *(Facing Page)*.
Photograph by George Cott

The client had admired a similar style of wood design in a European bistro and asked for a replication for his gentlemen's study. The weave of white oak and Brazilian mahogany was crafted into a rich wainscoting running throughout the room *(Above)*.
Photograph by George Cott

This striking element supports a handcrafted puzzle table designed by Robin Bell of Manhattan for one of America's most influential political families. The Hill Group master painstakingly applied the finish by hand through dozens of steps over a number of weeks *(Above)*.
Photograph by Rob Downey

Today, one of the foremost premier builders in northeast Florida, Ricardo (Dick) Morales Jr. began the company in the mid 1970s as a commercial real estate development venture, turning it into a very successful enterprise. By the mid 1980s, son Ricardo (Rick) Morales III was gaining critical experience in the large commercial sector of construction, which took him across the South and sharpened his insight and skills in construction management, as well as regional techniques.

Teaming up with his father, Rick expanded Morales Construction Company, which now incorporates both residential and light commercial building and also maintains a commercial real estate development division managed by brother-in-law T. Fitch King. The majority of the company's projects are high-end waterfront residences. While the most seasoned homeowners seek Morales Construction's services based on an impeccable reputation for delivering the highest quality home built "the right way," as well as from repeat referrals from prominent area architects including Richard Skinner, among others, it is the delivery of the home of their dreams that undoubtedly confirms their decision.

"Our building techniques and commitment to excellence are a family tradition."

~Rick Morales

MORALES CONSTRUCTION COMPANY, INC.

This Cape Cod, Shingle-style home was constructed for a very house-savvy couple—this is their eighth custom home. Because it is an oceanfront home and susceptible to the sometimes intensive conditions of the region, we incorporated many integral details such as German-made hurricane-protective windows from Tischler und Sohn. The red cedar shingles add to the charm and ease of sitting on this porch and enjoying the soft beach breeze. Interestingly, the flooring tile contains authentic fossils *(Previous Pages)*.
Photograph by Joe Lapeyra

A lovely view can be had from anywhere in this kitchen. The eye-catching mosaic wall tile sets the tone for the kitchen. To keep the walls light, uplights are placed in the white and glass cabinetry. Notice that countertops are brushed absolute black granite with a different polished granite on the island; it adds a bit of variety. Other beautiful elements include the custom built-in stainless surround in the stove area, quarter-sawn red oak floors and solid cypress beams *(Right)*.
Photograph by Joe Lapeyra

> "From millwork to tile flooring, we manage the operation of everything installed in our homes. We have a highly skilled team of expert craftsmen and subcontractors, many whom we have trusted for years."

~Rick Morales

The most notable aspect of this Jacksonville home on the St. John's River—from a construction perspective—is that all the white trim around the windows and home requires minimal maintenance, resisting mold and rot. We also added interest to an otherwise ignored piece of the home: the driveway. Brick pavers were accented by stained concrete *(Above)*.
Photograph by Joe Lapeyra

Again we see the fossilized tile flooring in this kitchen, which is from the house in the first photo. As in many beachfront homes, the desire of the kitchen was that it feel open and light. The slightly off-white cabinetry, multiple lighting options, and open access to the family room accomplish just that *(Facing Page Top)*.
Photograph by Joe Lapeyra

Again here, the real interest is in the craftsmanship of the mosaic tile flooring. Not only is it interesting, it is unexpected. The shower is absent of any lines in that it is a frameless glass enclosure and its entrance requires no step into, rather it is a rounded bottom which one walks into. We use this type of shower for aesthetic reasons but it is also ideal for a special needs situation *(Facing Page Bottom)*.
Photograph by Joe Lapeyra

"Our clients are very knowledgeable about what they want and what they don't want. They know quality and their high expectations always drive us to exceed all expectations."

~Rick Morales

Influenced by a Maine upbringing, the owner of this Georgian home desired a cupola on his roof with automatic nighttime lighting as viewed just above the dormer—classic of this particular genre. As mentioned before, we used the low maintenance synthetic trim here as well *(Above)*.
Photograph by Neil Rashba

The focal points of this cozy family room are the beautiful solid cypress beams as well as the pecky cypress over the fireplace. The natural finish of the woods complements and reinforces the flavor of the room which includes built-in bookcases and other unobtrusive details *(Facing Page)*.
Photograph by Joe Lapeyra

This photo gives a close-up view of white-washed brick, which "authenticates" this English-style cottage. The front solid beam is crafted of cypress and serves as the structure which holds the roof over the summer or outdoor kitchen *(Above)*.
Photograph by Joe Lapeyra

This photo highlights the level of small details—such as this trellis over the garage—which we incorporate into all of our homes *(Above)*.
Photograph by Joe Lapeyra

Since its founding in 1989, Newbury North Associates' exclusive focus has been concentrated on high-end, custom residential construction. They exact a level of excellence in detail unmatched in South Florida resulting in the finest quality of craftsmanship available. Owner David S. Rogers, a veteran of the residential construction industry in New England since 1980, launched Newbury North Associates more than 18 years ago after a visit to Naples when he discovered that the area offered a broader diversity of the clientele he wished to attract with his vast expertise, skills and industry relationships.

The company's impeccable reputation continues to grow among local and world-renowned architects, engineers and the most discriminating clientele. Newbury North has developed solid working relationships with trusted local and national subcontractors. Although the company has not sought recognition, publications such as *Architectural Digest* simply cannot resist the extraordinary residences with which Newbury North consistently continues to grace Florida's landscape.

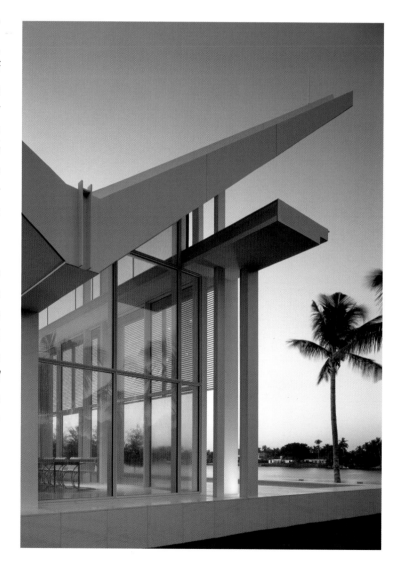

"Our clients and their architects seek a higher level of design and sophistication. No matter what style of architecture they are in, we make their dreams and passions ours and make it our goal to bring these to reality."

~David S. Rogers

NEWBURY NORTH ASSOCIATES

Designed by Richard Meier & Partners Architects of New York, this modern residence was built for a very discriminating European client. A hallmark of Richard Meier is the establishment of a precise grid, horizontally and vertically, within their overall designs. All elements of the project were based on the established grids. While beautifully subtle, one can notice the clean, easy definition of this in the finished residence. Richard Meier & Partners Architects does not address many single-family residential projects. Being called on to build this house presented a marvelous opportunity for our company to challenge itself with the diversity of the design. Primarily built of steel, stone and glass, the project's exacting tolerances left absolutely no allowance for deviation. The entire west face and each end were primarily built of glass supported by steel and aluminum horizontal and vertical members. The area of glass on the west face was approximately 180 feet long and over 20 feet tall. This, of course, presented the tremendous challenge of meeting the strenuous guidelines required to achieve the impact and wind load pressure required by southwest Florida. Not only was the glass curtain wall of the residence designed to meet the impact and wind load criteria, it was sent to a testing facility to prove it *(Previous Pages Left & Right)*.
Photography by Esto Photographics Inc.

The living/dining room of the home gives one a subtle feel of the established grids without the sense of rigidity. An outstanding quality of this home is the amazing play on natural light and shadows without glare even though the entire west face is glass. The introduction of rod-shaped louvers positioned off the curtain wall was a strong factor in providing for this. This project was a fine example of stellar communication and collaboration between the architect, builder, engineers and craftsmen. It required exemplary project management and focus from not only Newbury North but the tradespeople and craftsmen as well *(Right)*.
Photograph by Esto Photographics Inc.

Smith Architectural Group of Palm Beach designed this timeless Mediterranean-style residence with extraordinary detailing. Once again, collaboration and good communication from all parties was the key. The great hall displays some of the work of the fine national and international craftsmen who were brought in. The cast plaster columns, capitals and arched ceiling embellishments were custom designed and cast. A company from Canada carved, cast and installed this work as well as the architectural elements in many other rooms. The inlaid marble and limestone floor was custom designed by the architect and fabricated in Europe. The ornamental cast bronze and extruded bronze entrance door at the end of the hall was cast and built by a company in Utah *(Facing Page)*.

Photograph by Kim Sargent

Attention to detail was taken to another level on this home—first in design and second in the execution of the work. The house was set higher from the natural grade due to the coastal setting and state requirement. To complement the structure's height, battered walls at the base visually anchor the structure to the ground. True to the classic turn-of-the-century homes of Palm Beach, the majority of the exterior walls were clad in Florida coquina stone. The architect designed exquisite cast stone architectural elements to complement the coquina. From the terraces' finely detailed stone balustrades to the large yet perfectly scaled cornice that carries a different design depending on the area of the home, to the seven uniquely designed chimneys, the gulf view of this Mediterranean Italianate home demonstrates its impressive magnitude. The gulf

loggia has five 11-foot-tall arched openings that separate the loggia from the gulf terrace. When inclement weather tries to prevent the enjoyment of this space, the touch of a button raises hurricane-rated glass panels on elevator pistons from the basement and starts the air conditioning. Successfully completing this monumental project required a winning team on the construction side, which starts with the experienced Newbury North team and carefully assembled contractors and craftsmen. On top of this, you have to have a passion and a love for the work. I thoroughly enjoy the entire construction process from start to finish. I especially enjoy being on site with my people, analyzing construction details and methodologies, and assuring the highest level of quality is achieved in every aspect *(Above)*.

Photograph by Kim Sargent

The main staircase in the residence, clad completely in French limestone, winds up the circular walls of the stair hall. The ornate finely detailed bronze rails wrap the stairs tying in the shadows of the custom bronze skylight, bringing in natural lights to the hall *(Left)*.
Photograph by Kim Sargent

The older home that previously stood on the property had an old pond. Our client, whom we had previously built a home for, always liked the pond. His vision was to recreate the pond, make it larger and connect it to the walls of the house and to be able to create a bridge to access the main motor court. Magnificent detail does not stop at the house. The arches of the bridge are clad with coquina and overlaid with cast stone mouldings. To keep the feel of the bridge open yet safe at the same time, concrete steel reinforced ballards were poured and then encased with a tapered cast stone cladding visually supported by beautiful carved and cast brackets. Custom designed bronzed chain and anchors were cast and installed to make the guard rail complete. The previously shown modern home and this Mediterranean-style residence demonstrate diversity in design yet both highlight the need for exacting attention to detail and craftsmanship *(Facing Page)*.
Photograph by Kim Sargent

"One of the highlights of building high-end custom residences is not only working with our wonderful clients but being able to work for talented architects on the truly unique and beautiful designs as well as diverse styles of architecture. We continually must rise to meet each challenge that a project presents."

~David S. Rogers

t was a simple ad in the newspaper that enticed Linda Pellegrini to make a surprising career change from the world of education into the construction industry. A custom home builder was looking specifically for a teacher's critical organizational and people skills to translate well as its construction superintendent. The risky career change paid off for Linda who went on to become owner and president of Allendale Custom Homes, which changed its name to Pellegrini Homes, Inc. in 1989.

Truly a custom home builder, Pellegrini Homes graces the most prominent communities in Florida with its powerful presence. Though the projects of this "First Lady of Home Building" are found in the most prestigious communities, it is not prestige she seeks; that has merely been the result of Linda and her team's commitment to building the most superior quality homes possible. Communication with her team and the client is key to each home's success. Linda attends meetings, visits sites weekly and is involved in every one of her company's projects. It is a service industry in the truest sense, and Linda and her team never forget that a job well done for them results in a haven and place of memories for their clients.

"Building a home should be an enjoyable, exciting process for everyone involved. We want our clients to have as much fun as we do."

~Linda Pellegrini

PELLEGRINI HOMES

"This industry affords me the tremendous opportunity to translate something intangible into a beautiful, three-dimensional masterpiece."

~Linda Pellegrini

A Tuscan-style residence in the prestigious Isleworth development of Central Florida, this home is beautifully mirrored in "Hourglass Lake" beyond. The architect, Terry Irwin, designed the home to reflect the elegance of a country home in Tuscany with lush, manicured gardens. As stunning as the home is on the outside, it is equally impressive inside with luxurious decorative interior elements. This primary home, owned by an active, young family, boasts a half basketball court, lap pool and has a detached guest house on the property as well *(Previous Pages)*.
Photograph by © Raymond Martinot

This dining room was featured in one of our Street of Dreams Showhouses located in Lake Nona Estates Golf Club, and was designed by architect Mark Nasrallah. The room is actually an open space whose interior boundaries are designated by stately pre-cast stone columns. The vibrantly faux-painted walls and architectural details make the room a lovely and elegant gathering place *(Right)*.
Photograph courtesy of Pellegrini Homes, Inc.

The first of the next three photos located in the first home shown, this great room reflects an elegant yet functional space for the whole family. Overhead, cypress planks and beams have been hand painted and sandblasted for an authentic aged appearance anchored by iron ties, which complete the look. The focal point of the room is the large fireplace mantel and flanking columns—hand carved of Mexican limestone marble—further enhanced by the stone and wood floor and custom cabinetry of the room's surroundings. As the heart of the home, this living space is the first thing seen upon entering the home and we made it special yet functional *(Facing Page Top)*.

This entrance gallery leads from the foyer to the master suite beyond the ornately designed gate. What you cannot see is the corridor effect created by the groin vaults at either end of the gallery. The elements in the gallery include Venetian plaster walls and ceiling, carved wall brackets and six medallions of marble and granite retrieved from the Vatican in Rome *(Facing Page Bottom Left)*.

The faux-painted detail of the master bathroom's ceiling is ingeniously mirrored in the hand-laid mosaic tiling on the floor. The distressed maple vanities, topped by Rojo Alacante marble, "float" in the room creating privacy to the shower and tub while allowing movement through the space *(Facing Page Bottom Right)*.

A Tuscan villa creates an inviting approach with warm hues and an impressive front elevation. The gold and black railing along sweeping stairs adds drama and additional interest. The gated drive provides privacy to courtyard balconies and railings pre-cast with aluminum inserts *(Above)*.
Photography courtesy of Pellegrini Homes, Inc.

"Nothing evidences a job well done better than a smile."

~Linda Pellegrini

This kitchen, with a distinct Tuscan villa flavor, appeared in the Lake Nona Showhouse. Noticeable at once are three different diverse, yet complementary wood selections: aged cream, natural maple and terracotta. The walls have been faux painted with copper accents. The cypress wood ceiling, with crown moulding and small stone decorative corbels, truly confirms the intended flavor of the room *(Facing Page)*.

Additional details of the Lake Nona Showhouse: The curved cove detail of the master bedroom ceiling extended over the drapery to the door. Artistry by Sarah Pelfrey of Artisan Inc. *(Top Left)*.

In the vestibule, this crown moulding, glazed with a silver and gold leaf decorative paint treatment, focuses on the light. Artistry by Sarah Pelfrey of Artisan Inc. *(Top Right)*.

The reeds found in a pond along the property provided inspiration for this pool house bathroom's stained glass images *(Bottom Left)*.

Arched entrance column and element *(Bottom Right)*. *Photography courtesy of Pellegrini Homes, Inc.*

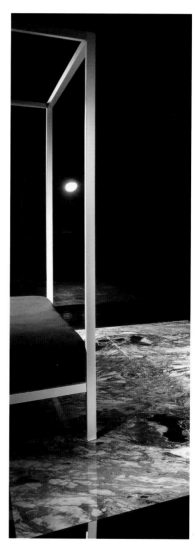

Mystic Granite & Marble, *Page 101*   Tischler und Sohn, *Page 111*

elements of structure

chapter three

Architectural Artworks Incorporated, *Page 121*

SAFE, *Page 139*

Amazon Metal Fabricators, *Page 151*

"Starting with a few employees and working from my kitchen table, my vision of Mystic Granite & Marble became a reality with our new 70,000-square-foot facility. Today we are one of the largest distributors of natural stone tile and slab in the southeast, working with a range of projects from residential to commercial skyscrapers."

~Darlene Spezzi

Nature's elements of sunlight and stone combine to enhance the beauty of this translucent light green onyx. The large framed panels offer added drama in this commercial application *(Facing Page)*. *Photograph by Corey Alexander, Mystic Granite & Marble*

Customers who enter Mystic's Design Center and Showroom are welcomed by a custom logo mosaic crafted from a variety of granites, marbles and other complementary natural stones *(Above)*. *Photograph by Beth Dover, Mystic Granite & Marble*

"For our residential and commercial clients alike, not only granite but all natural stone material, such as travertine, marble and onyx, have surged in popularity as trends toward personal style and self-expression have quickly emerged."

~Darlene Spezzi

Dramatic hues of soft green from this exotic Irish Green marble provide spa ambience in this upscale home *(Above Left)*.
Photograph by Antolini Luigi

Old World aesthetic meets contemporary design in this elegant and dynamic commercial staircase. Verde Fantastico marble takes the simplicity of a stairway and creates a haven of passage *(Above Right)*.
Photograph by Antolini Luigi

This dream-like corridor features meticulously book-and-diamond matched slabs of Irish Green marble. Mosaic tiles frame the architectural features of this custom space *(Facing Page)*.
Photograph by Antolini Luigi

"My passion is to show our clients the beauty and durability of natural stone, maybe consider a color or pattern they never even thought about."

~Darlene Spezzi

The distinct color palette of gold and silver gives this homeowner a signature look of ultra contemporary design *(Facing Page)*.
Photograph by Antolini Luigi

Handmade medallions can be customized to complement any residential or commercial application. Mosaic design process has evolved over centuries of time; from handmade tile mosaics to today's high-tech water jet design method *(Above)*.
Photography courtesy of Mystic Granite & Marble

"Always select your natural stone first, then choose your paint color, fabrics and cabinet color to blend with the natural stone color. You can always change the paint, fabrics and cabinet colors but you can't change the color of your stone."

~Darlene Spezzi

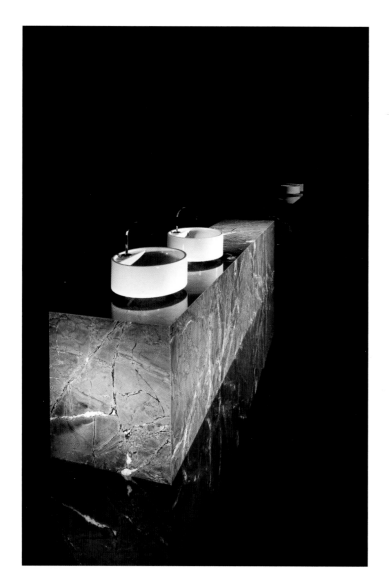

To dream it is to design it in the world of natural stone. This master bath is a focal point of the home using Verde Fantastico marble as a major design element *(Facing Page Left)*.
Photograph by Antolini Luigi

Small panels of Green Bowenite "Dark" Serpentine combine with spot lighting to create a comfortable ambience in this office waiting room *(Facing Page Right)*.
Photograph by Antolini Luigi

Relax in this villa with diamond-matched Irish Green marble *(Above)*.
Photograph by Antolini Luigi

"Nothing is as satisfying as seeing the 'wow look' come across the clients' faces when they fall in love with the unique stone that will be the centerpiece in their home. Every stone is like a piece of artwork—no two pieces are alike."

~Darlene Spezzi

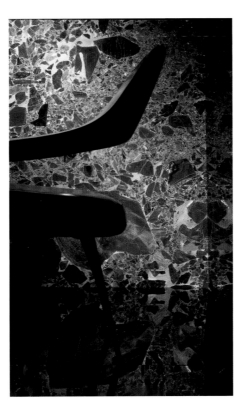

Exotic and semi-precious stones are the most highly desired materials in high-end design *(Above)*.
Photograph by Antolini Luigi

Breche de Vendome is one of nature's most fascinating and aesthetically rich natural stones. This application demonstrates how stone can be considered a piece of art *(Facing Page)*.
Photograph by Antolini Luigi

This close-up of Black Beauty granite shows amazing detail *(Above)*.
Photograph by Antolini Luigi

Brown petrified wood slab: a miracle of nature achieved by blending together the unique beauty of multicolored minerals cast in petrified wood with highly skilled craftsmanship *(Above)*.
Photograph by Antolini Luigi

"Creating ultra-high-end doors and windows that are equally durable and aesthetically appealing is truly rewarding, because we know that the recipients of our custom-manufactured products will enjoy them well into the future."

~Timothy Carpenter

The superior quality of our products is matched only by the caliber of service we offer, and we don't leave the installation to just anyone. Whether the project is in Aspen, Tokyo, Moscow, Sardinia, the Caribbean or Naples, Florida, like this magnificent home, our professionals personally see to it that the job is done right. As is demonstrated here by the variety of window and door shapes and sizes, we have the capability to manufacture products of virtually any dimension—architects fully appreciate the creative flexibility that working with us affords. We use only the highest quality, most durable wood to ensure that our products—which can withstand wind speeds in excess of 140 miles per hour—will not twist or warp, shrink or swell in intense sunlight, high humidity or dreadful rain. The richly stained mahogany doors and windows nicely complement the limestone and stucco exterior, designed by Stofft Cooney Architects *(Facing Page & Above)*.
Photography courtesy of Stofft Cooney Architects

"An architect's vision should not be limited by what kinds of windows and doors can be found in a catalog. We work closely with architects in order to achieve highly engineered, custom solutions which will satisfy their most discerning patrons."

~James Myers

When Palm Beach's town hall, a landmark historical building, underwent an extensive renovation, the architectural firm Digby Bridges & Marsh enlisted our services to grace the structure with windows and doors of the highest quality. Framed with Sipo mahogany—the most durable outdoor-use wood, second only to teak—our superb products will last a lifetime. *(Facing Page)*.
Photograph courtesy of Digby Bridges & Marsh

Designed by Richard Skinner & Associates, this home is located in the seaside community of Ponte Vedra. Serene views are enjoyed through the double-hung and handcrafted oval windows in this formal, yet intimate library setting *(Above Left)*.
Photograph courtesy of Richard Skinner & Associates

A custom combination of roll-down screens and light diffusing and blackout shades was employed for this beachfront residence. The window screens are securely locked into their tracks to withstand even the strongest winds *(Above Right)*.
Photograph courtesy of Richard Skinner & Associates

This Mediterranean-style Digby Bridges & Marsh creation in Palm Beach features 10-foot-high French doors which are topped with three-foot half-round transoms. We are not only a source for custom doors and windows but also a resource. Architects and builders rely on our expertise from the outset of their projects. We collaborate with and advise them as to how we can best meet each project's unique needs. Here, we've matched the residence's timeless elegance by blending the wood frames into the façade, rather than using them to punctuate the design. Just as with all of our products, the doors and windows of this exquisite residence were manufactured in Germany by skilled journeymen in a temperature- and humidity-regulated environment. Precision is not achieved with a mere ruler, but rather through the employment of cutting-edge technology, guaranteeing accuracy to the millimeter *(Left)*.
Photograph courtesy of Digby Bridges & Marsh

"From penthouses in Manhattan to chalets in Kitzbuhel, estates in Connecticut and villas in Sardinia, our clients' projects literally span the world."

~Steve Albert

Though the windows in the circular architectural element of this Spanish Revival-style are not actually curved, we do have the capability to construct curved windows and doors and have done so on many occasions *(Facing Page Top)*.
Photograph courtesy of Digby Bridges & Marsh

Rather than specifying windows and doors that would disappear into the architecture, the architects of Digby Bridges & Marsh used our windows and doors to their full potential in this residence. The custom-stained, solid mahogany door with glass accents serves as a focal point of the gracious loggia. The in-swing and out-swing windows' wood frames have been stained to match *(Facing Page Center & Bottom)*.
Photography courtesy of Digby Bridges & Marsh

Willing and able to match any stain or paint color, all of our products are completely factory-finished. The custom finish of this Spanish Revival home's window and door frames was tested for its ability to withstand ultraviolet radiation, rain, acid rain, dirt and myriad other forces of nature. Our application process has been carefully developed over the course of many decades; it ensures that the coating, be it stain or paint, does not peel, chip or fade unnecessarily *(Above)*.
Photograph courtesy of Digby Bridges & Marsh

"When people want the best, they come to us."

~Timothy Carpenter

Designed by Mark P. Finlay Architects, AIA, this majestic low-country estate, located outside of Charleston, South Carolina, has more than 100 windows and doors of varying shapes and sizes. The energy-efficient windows, all of which are hurricane compliant, were employed to allow spectacular views and to balance the residence's proportions. A bank of curved glass was specified on the left side of the first-level veranda *(Facing Page Top)*.
Photograph by Durston Saylor

This Mark P. Finlay Architect design was featured in the July 2007 issue of *Architectural Digest*. The Charleston home's living room illustrates Tischler products at their best. A series of perfectly proportioned French doors with richly stained wood frames connect the inside spaces with nature *(Facing Page Bottom)*.
Photograph by Durston Saylor

The interior architecture of this South Carolina residence mimics the exterior. Even the kitchen cabinetry echoes the architectural grace of the large custom windows. Designed by the architects of Shope Reno Wharton, the home features an elegant, triangular-shaped window, demonstrative of our wide-ranging capabilities *(Above)*.
Photography by Dickson Dunlap

ARCHITECTURAL ARTWORKS INCORPORATED

This contemporary-styled kitchen display is highlighted on our showroom floor. We feel it is important for our clients to touch and feel potential materials and finishes that will eventually become part of their kitchen. The vignette has been designed with an intentional mix of high-end materials to give clients exposure to several choices that will guide and inform their decisions. The lavastone tabletop, in brilliant turquoise, with an inset of mother-of-pearl and paua shell mosaics is set off by the neutral tones of the materials that surround it in the display. The adjacent, taller island countertop is made of concrete inset with semi-precious gemstones and a sink cover of aroko wood. The countertop above the perimeter base cabinets is a burgundy slate while the floor is glass terrazzo. Cherry veneer cabinetry has been treated with a high-gloss finish on the island and matte finish on the perimeter *(Facing Page)*.
Photograph by Everett & Soule

The two-tone design of this kitchen evokes pure, modern elegance. The traditional kitchen has evolved into a contemporary, multi-functional and open living space. Floating shelves with ample storage space provide options to showcase or store china while carriers organize kitchen essentials out of sight. Dominant design features include the obsidian smoked glass set against warm shimmering walnut combined with smooth sterling grey matte lacquered surfaces. Together they create a warm ambience and a flowing transition between the kitchen and living areas *(Above)*.
Photograph courtesy of Architectural Artworks Inc.

"Architectural Artworks and our clients work closely together sharing a mutually deep appreciation for quality and excellence."

~Joan DesCombes

This kitchen personifies the use of "reductionist aesthetic" at its best. This intended result is meant to integrate living spaces with an open kitchen, thereby maximizing the feeling of spaciousness in a smaller area while also emphasizing a reduced overall design. One can observe how the accessibility of the eating area acts as an extension of the kitchen. Clean lines and materials of stainless steel, granite and dark woods create an elegant and refined integration in the living area of the home. Special attention to detail was paid to the countertops, which were hand-laid in a tiny stone and gemstone mosaic design *(Facing Page)*.

Photograph courtesy of Architectural Artworks Inc.

We designed and executed the installation of this kitchen for a client who observably has a love for color and was not afraid to let her kitchen reflect that. The overall design incorporates minimalist forms and clean, simple lines. Desiring to keep her cabinetry neutral with a color "pop," she chose this vibrant yellow lavastone backsplash and countertop complemented by apple green wall color. The yellow is incorporated in the stove hood using a strip that glows when the lights are off. Modern elm emulation finish wood cabinetry gives the illusion of a much more expansive space. Use of contemporary appliances and a fully integrated refrigerator complete the necessary elements in keeping with the artistic influence. Demi tall cabinets guarantee no clutter in the small but well-planned workspace. Further concealing any clutter is a roll-top tambour which conceals a television, telephone and small appliances. Finally, an island peninsula creates a visual divide between the kitchen and living areas *(Above)*.

Photograph by Everett & Soule

"By whatever means it is achieved, art is in the hand and eye of the maker—where it then moves to the eye of the beholder."

~Roland DesCombes

Designed by Roland DesCombes, this opulent two-story library was created to reflect the homeowner's request for a quiet reading retreat. Conscious of the desire for both beauty and function, the space includes expansive display space in rich, walnut-paneled walls which have been enhanced with classic dentil moulding. The heavily coffered ceiling offers an additional eye-pleasing effect while a spiral staircase curves elegantly upward to a catwalk allowing access to the second-story book shelves. The crowning design element is a heavily carved wooden fireplace surround featuring sculptural human figures *(Facing Page)*.
Photograph by Phil Eschbach

The new owner of this kitchen opted to tear out the existing kitchen in an effort to transform it into her vision of a more functional, attractive space that flowed into a large breakfast and family room. The feel of the new space combines eclectic elements and the owner's collectibles, transforming it into a classic American High-Country style. Freestanding furniture pieces have been included in the room: an armoire that houses the refrigerator, a small worktable at the foot of the island that combines marble and butcher block surfaces, and a blue-painted larder. The look is carried through in the blending of cabinetry finishes as well, from the hand-painted white-glazed wall and base cabinets to the darker-tone stained, antiqued island. We were also able to capture the owner's expressed wish to have fresh herbs available in her kitchen through the use of an herb garden complete with a built-in drain. The eclectic space fulfills the owner's desire for the perfect blending of casual elegant styling with detailed functionality *(Above)*.
Photograph by Everett & Soule

"Having a staff of talented in-house tile designers and our own team of highly experienced installers sets Island Tile & Stone apart from other tile companies."

~Laurie Fourmont

This bathroom was created for the home of award-winning builders Mark and Beth McIntosh. Above the Sonoma cast-stone, double-wave sink are two mirrors that reflect the "star attraction" of the bathroom—the shower. Designed for their son, an avid surfer, this whimsical beach scene thoroughly personalizes the bathroom *(Facing Page)*.

Up close, one can see the playful interaction of color in this exuberant mosaic. Our staff takes pleasure in creating works of art in unexpected places *(Above)*.
Photography by Rixon Photography, LLC

"In addition to tile and stone we also carry a fine selection of specialty sinks, ranging from earthy concrete farmhouse sinks to colorful hand painted vessels."

~Laurie Fourmont

This elegant powder room features a stone vessel sink, tumbled marble wainscoting and stone banding. The basket-weave flooring represents our commitment to excellence in that each tiny piece of interlocking marble was painstakingly fabricated and hand laid by our craftsmen (Left).

This is a wet bar in the kitchen of the same home. The unique hand-painted tumbled marble mural was commissioned by Island Tile & Stone. This backsplash is a favorite of the homeowners as it recalls warm memories and cheerful times; the champagne bottle in the mural is a replica of the one enjoyed at their wedding (Facing Page Left).

A close-up of the mural reveals bottles of the couple's favorite wines. We encourage our clients to explore the bounds of creativity with their choices; there are endless possibilities to personalize their tile work (Facing Page Top & Bottom Right).
Photography by Robert Downey

"My inspiration to open a high-end tile and stone showroom came while traveling throughout Europe and experiencing breathtaking stonework and tile work—historic and contemporary—firsthand. I wanted to open a showroom with an outstanding collection of artisan tile and luxury stone that would provide aesthetic creativity, durability and design flexibility."

~Laurie Fourmont

"We help our clients select colors, textures and an overall tile design scheme that complements the style of their home."

~Laurie Fourmont

A serene and uplifting bathroom incorporates a neutral palette including a countertop of tumbled marble and Jerusalem limestone flooring complemented by mosaic inserts. The shower features Egyptian limestone walls and a mosaic band that seamlessly ties the look together. Island Tile & Stone imports exotic stone for authenticity and quality that are hard to surpass (Facing Page).

The subtle elegance of the Jerusalem limestone is a perfect backdrop for the living room of this spectacular home. The diagonal layout of the stone flooring gently guides the eye towards the breathtaking water view (Above Left).

The kitchen fulfills the desire for a light and airy quality throughout the home. The stunning granite countertops and backsplash of tumbled Jerusalem mosaic provide a tranquil setting and the perfect ambience for entertaining (Above Right).
Photography by Robert Downey

OLDE WORLD CABINETRY

Largo, FL

This beautiful Mediterranean kitchen was crafted by a detail-oriented builder with whom we often work. As in most of our new design projects, we were brought in to consult with the clients and builder during the planning stages. From the initial meetings, it was apparent that the husband loves to cook and the couple enjoys entertaining. Therefore, the kitchen was designed around these two criteria. Appliances were strategically placed to allow the homeowners to cook while interacting with their guests. Custom-designed glazed cherry wood cabinets with five-step crown moulding detail continue the space's splendor. This kitchen won the Regional and Grand Aurora Award from The International Home Builders Conference, but more importantly, the homeowners are delighted with it *(Facing Page)*.

This kitchen remodel was for a condominium in the historic Bayfront Towers in downtown St. Petersburg. The clients are a well traveled couple, recently married, with a wonderful art collection. Both have amazing taste as well as worldly and exquisite design sensibility. The entire décor of the home was designed around a Dale Chihuly painting, so the kitchen was kept contemporary and neutral with clean lines *(Above Left)*.

The fabulous Ann Sachs tile was discovered by the homeowner. It creates an artful "pop" in the kitchen and complements the Chihuly piece. The interesting, frosted glass shelf above the tile provides additional indirect lighting. Although the kitchen is compact, it is efficient and, as a result of the color palette and light, appears larger than it actually is *(Above Right)*. *Photography by Rixon Photography, LLC*

"I am driven by the desire to create something useful as well as totally individual, distinctive, timeless and beautiful."

~Nancy Braamse

This beach house was built as a family retreat for a major developer in the Tampa/St. Petersburg area. The bathroom was designed for his young sons. In keeping with the beach theme of the house, the countertop is a manmade product intended to resemble beach glass. Although this is a small space, it works exactly as intended and still stays beachy and fun *(Facing Page Top)*.

The one-piece glass sink and countertop in the house's powder room is embedded with color that creates an informally elegant ambience for the space *(Facing Page Bottom)*.

The homeowners' desire for functionality in this kitchen was family focused. They wanted to be able to cook and interact with their young children at the same time. So, the space was designed with seating around the perimeter where the children could be seen yet safely out from underfoot. To carry the color palette from the rest of the house into the kitchen, a two and a half inch thick Bahia blue granite countertop with fractured edge was introduced for the island. The cabinetry is horizontal-grain anigre wood. The perimeter countertops are a manmade quartz product honed to resemble the appearance of beach sand. Location definitely inspired the design of this home—and kitchen—a wonderful project *(Above)*.

Photography by Rixon Photography, LLC

"Exceeding my customers' expectations is my passion ... the end result is their dreams."

~Nancy Braamse

A "his and hers" master bath/closet was the focus of this project. Shown here is "her" bathroom, dressing room and beautiful closet. The primary design criteria for this space was that it be a place with a spa-like serenity for rest and re-energizing. An elegant woman, this client's design choices were as equally sophisticated as they were timelessly classic. The cabinetry is custom crafted of stained and glazed alder wood, while the floor is heated granite tiles *(Facing Page)*.

A close-up view of a hand-carved angel graces either side of the "retreat's" shower door *(Right)*. *Photography by Rixon Photography, LLC*

SAFE
STRATEGICALLY ARMORED & FORTIFIED ENVIRONMENTS

Los Angeles, CA

"In today's world, the safety of one's family is no longer an assurance but rather a proactive pursuit that can only be attained through careful planning."

~Al Corbi

From a splendid and inviting spiral staircase with intelligence that monitors friend-or-foe activity and responds accordingly, to a beautifully handcrafted vanity that transforms itself into the nerve center of one of the most significant estates in America; things are rarely what they appear in a SAFE home ... *(Facing Page & Above)*.

State-of-the-art surveillance keeps you in touch with your properties and loved ones without the necessity of computer access from the above touch panel or remotely from around the world ... regardless of how far from home your travels may take you *(Above Left)*.

SAFE's Access Control System provides unparalleled remote status and locking control from the above touch panel—providing its owner the ability to monitor every door and window, observe every acre of land, and control any threat that might befall his family—from within an impenetrable ballistic Safe Core™ *(Above Right)*.
Photography by www.lendepasphoto.com

"No one wins in a fight. There are only varying degrees of loss. Time, not force, is the critical factor to ensure a safe outcome. Time eventually neutralizes any threat, while force raises the stakes, typically increasing the danger. SAFE's systems isolate your family from the threat until it is neutralized and they can't be harmed."

~Al Corbi

When the requirement to "Protect What Matters Most" goes beyond the safety of one's family, SAFE's world-class security solutions go beyond "the stuff movies are made of." To house and protect an important contemporary automobile collection I created the ultimate secure solution: A world-class, real-life Bat Cave. The biometrically controlled waterfall, massive ballistic grade doors, retractable steel ramp and koi-filled moat discourage uninvited callers. Elevated platforms inside the Bat Cave display the automobiles while providing an additional level of security, restricting their ability to be moved. Sensory and tactical systems provide the final level of assurance that the cars will remain safe and sound. SAFE likens its high-tech measures to the spare tire in your car. You hope you never need it, but would you really want to go down the road without it? *(Facing Page & Above)*.
Renderings by Ricardo Perez

"For security to be effective it must be invisible. One can't defeat what can't be seen … and there is nothing more intimidating than the unknown."

~Al Corbi

Discreet passageways and hidden vaults reside within Safe Cores™, an innovation which I pioneered. Safe Cores are created by combining multiple rooms into an impenetrable core. In the event of a threat, residents remain safe, comfortable and in control *(Facing Page & Bottom Right)*.

SAFE's integrators have mastered the art of embedding its highly developed systems into the most sophisticated interiors with little or no sign of their existence. The outdoor lighting pictured features the highest level of day/night surveillance, which locks onto an intruder, tracks and records their every move *(Top Right)*.

Photography by www.lendepasphoto.com

"We have not changed our methods of hand craftsmanship and innovative design since our grandfather founded the company. Every aspect in the creation of our metalwork is done on-site, in our shop and by hand—the traditional way."

~Joe Ponsler

This ornate main stair railing was crafted for our clients to complement their exceptionally formal French Normandy residence. As are all of our designs, this is an original design—crafted in-house—and incorporates 23-karat gilding over antiqued steel with capped railing. The bottom terminus demonstrates where the skill and experience of hand craftsmanship are critical: It flows without the appearance of being forced *(Facing Page)*.

An entry gate is a welcoming point and the first impression guests see when they enter the property. As one can see from the matching elements in the railing (shown at left), the style was continued here for the same residence. Our exterior work goes through a rigorous sand-blasting, metallizing and painting process to ensure aesthetic integrity as well as the prevention of rust for years to come *(Above)*.
Photography by Daryl Bunn

"We measure our success by the delight of our clients and also by the respect and admiration of our peers."

~James Ponsler

Designed for an English-style home, this main stair railing encompasses forged steel mounts to panels that require exact placement on the treads. It incorporates elements of steel with copper and brass details *(Facing Page Top & Center)*.

This is the "kick plate" of a wine cellar gate in the same French Normandy residence. The cellar has a "castle-like," Neo-Gothic quality. In order to adopt the aura of the space, the gate incorporates rivets, heavy details and piercing *(Bottom)*.

Photography by Daryl Bunn

Because this is such an eclectic home, it called for a very unique design. The homeowners hail from different ethnicities and this appealed to both tastes— a design that was actually inspired by a photo in a magazine which we took to another level by personalizing it for the couple *(Above)*.

These photos show the level of detail and time we incorporate into our work. In the same staircase (shown above), the bronze center is crafted in metal repoussé inspired by antique leaves *(Facing Page)*.
Photography by Daryl Bunn

"We are proud of our heritage—from Wonderland's beginning over 50 years ago as a small Jacksonville crafter of playground equipment (hence the name), to our evolution as a high-end residential producer of superior metal railings, entry gates and more all over the United States and beyond."

~Bob Ponsler

"Paint and curtains can easily be changed; metal work is permanent. We understand and respect the importance of our clients' projects."

~Don Benson

The owners of this home are originally from Germany and own a brewery. Their tastes reflect a Medieval influence as seen in their home which resembles a castle. They desired an original staircase railing design which would carry the look and complement their home's unique style. The three-story circular railing, punctuated by trapezoidal columns, was comprised of steel which was forged and punched through to maintain the integrity of the structure. The result is a solid and stately appearance. We, and they, feel it makes quite a statement *(Facing Page)*.

Here, a decorative railing was desired to complement a Spanish-style home's exterior circular stair. The railing was hand forged in our company's on-site metal working facility and crafted of aluminum. For exterior work such as this, the proper alloy of aluminum is critical and this particular metal is the one of choice for its ability to withstand corrosive weathering *(Above)*.
Photography courtesy of Amazon Metal Fabrication

"We work with our clients to deliver the best design according to their unique stylistic tastes and functional needs. Our work stands the test of time both artistically and structurally."

~Don Benson

There is much more than meets the eye in creating estate gates. Along with aesthetic beauty, structural rigidity, site of gate and wind resistance must all be considered and factored in that particular gate's construction. This gate required the perfect balance between structural and architectural aluminum *(Facing Page Left)*.

This aluminum railing serves as a very important design element for this home. It is the first thing viewed upon entering the home and sets the tone for the entire estate which recalls refined Old World elegance. The ornate railing involved quite an evolution in design as the homeowners began the process with a completely different idea in mind. Our commitment to our clients finds us in this similar scenario quite often, but we believe in the importance of our product because we are creating permanent design elements *(Facing Page Top)*.

This hand-forged, wrought iron front-door scrollwork beautifully alters the look of this traditional glass and wood door, adding interest and elegance to an otherwise basic front door *(Facing Page Bottom)*.

These clients desired a definite departure from the "traditional" in their residence. This crosshatch railing follows a curved staircase and as in all of our metal work, required exacting measurements and craftsmanship *(Right)*.
Photography courtesy of Amazon Metal Fabrication

GET ORGANIZED, INC.

Orlando, FL

We designed and created this closet for The New American Home project presented by the Home Builders Association. We were honored to work on this particular project as the builder and craftspeople are chosen by the Association rather than bidding for it. The closet makes the most of its space with handcrafted natural maple storage cabinets and a granite-top island with multiple pull-out drawers. For a functional as well as a decorative appearance, glass has been placed in the cabinet doors, which display lit rods. Amenities include a washer and dryer and concealed ironing board. We handcrafted all the woodwork, including the doors and crown moulding, using state-of-the-art equipment and technology at our on-site 20,000-square-foot facility *(Facing Page)*.

I don't know a single person who wouldn't be impressed—even rendered speechless—by this extraordinary closet, which is well over 1,000 square feet at two stories high. Built by preeminent Orlando custom home builder Southpoint Custom Homes, this was actually a spec home built to exceed very high expectations. In all of our projects, we are inspired by the homeowners' desires, tone, theme and style of the home as well as what our research reveals. As this home did not have an owner, we were inspired by the theme of the home and incorporated it into the closet design carrying out the turnkey process. Nothing was left out of this closet, which even features a breakfast bar. We chose to use back-lit, obscured inlaid glass doors to complement the elegance found throughout the home *(Above)*.
Photography by Joe Miller

"Our success is predicated by the utilization of our design team's intensive collaboration of ideas, philosophies and creativity to produce an innovative approach to elegant style, which is specifically tailored to each client's lifestyle, business and budget."

~Ben Benkiran

This kitchen is located in part of our showroom. The cabinetry is made of maple wood in which we made our own box cuts and handcrafted everything from scratch, including the mouldings. The kitchen design facet of our company has been such a thriving part of our business. We recently opened our new company, Park Avenue Kitchen Design Group, which is devoted solely to kitchen planning, design and installation *(Facing Page)*.

We paneled this rich, sophisticated theater—for a well-known sports celebrity—in mahogany with complementary mahogany medallions in gilded leafing. Guests are delighted to find that one of the panels is actually a secret door which leads onto the balcony *(Top)*.

We designed and built this home office for an attorney. Obviously created for the display and storage of many books, this is also a serene and equally handsome space to work within. To add design interest, the corner shelving features up-lit glass doors where the client has displayed a collection of airplane models *(Bottom)*.
Photography by Joe Miller

Viewed from the tasting room, this stunning wine cellar was handcrafted out of antiqued and distressed butternut and completed with a meticulously hand-rubbed French finish. The hand-scraped, custom-finish walnut flooring of the tasting room transitions into the imported tile flooring of the cellar. Once through the ornate iron-grated door, a fully functional bar, as well as banquettes for additional seating, are in view. The ornate crown mouldings, imported from England, as well as the sophisticated carvings and capitals, are finished in a striking hand-finished gold leaf, further elevating the level of sophistication and desired atmosphere of the space. At about 700 square feet, this room was designed to hold approximately 1,800 bottles and has various display niches complete with uplights to focus on cherished labels. The entire Hyland team is particularly proud of the work in this room as they all had a very integral role in its craftsmanship *(Facing Page)*.
Photograph by Brynn Bruijn

This family room entertainment center is crafted of dyed birdseye maple and was designed to display not only artful pieces valuable to the clients, but the television and the audio system for the entire house as well. The piece's frame and drawer fronts are made of contrasting teak which incorporates the wood palette of the teak office (shown left) of the same house. The frame is suspended away from back panels for a "floating" illusion *(Above Left)*.
Photograph by Tom Harper

"We pride ourselves on creating unique, one-of-a-kind pieces. Nothing our clients dream is out of reach."

~Rob Rieland

The interior of this office was crafted of teak, giving the room a rich tone, which would reflect the "Contemporary Tropical" feel of the home's décor. In lieu of a traditional door, a pocket door entryway with a shutter design was created, giving the homeowners the option to shut the office off from the family room for privacy or when not in use, yet leaves the doors as an integral part of the room. Inside the office, space was maximized with adequate shelving that would give the clients a place to display the treasures wrought from their many travels *(Previous Page Above Right)*.
Photograph by Tom Harper

Located in a condominium, this Transitional living room called for a fireplace surround that would be contemporary and unique. Crafted of Macassar ebony wood, the surround was fitted with adequate display shelving and a round mirror *(Above Left)*.
Photograph by Randall Perry Photography

This master bedroom (located in the same condominium as the fireplace surround) piece complements the Transitional décor and wood tone of the living room. This built-in functions as a storage chest as well as a way to display various curios. Two woods were used: a dark wood, custom stained African Sapele and a light wood, East Indian Rosewood, to design this completely one-of-a-kind piece *(Above Right)*.
Photograph by Randall Perry Photography

"We work as a true team, placing no more value on one person's contribution over another. Each member of the Hyland team is essential to the superior work we do."

~Chris Hylemon

In keeping with the light décor of this East Hampton vacation home, the natural finish of the furniture-style bathroom vanity allows the grain and character to truly come through. Furniture-style pieces are highly desired and can be accommodated in the kitchen, bathroom and bedroom; anywhere the client desires. This piece was custom designed in Naples and then shipped to the Manhattan-based client *(Right).*
Photograph by Susan Boyd

KLAHM & SONS

Ocala, FL

"Since our company's founding in 1972, it has always been our belief that your mind is your limitation when it comes to the possibilities of metalwork."

~Jack Klahm

This dramatic staircase is made exceptionally elegant with a custom-designed railing. The traditional style of the graceful wave design, featuring the bronze acanthus leaves, supports a continuous fluidity. We designed the railing so that the spheres would "float" on the leaves rather than be anchored by rails. Although, it's stressed often by many craftsmen, good design is truly in the details in our work *(Facing Page)*.
Photograph by Mark Baret

This entry gate greets the residents of the immaculate 1,000-acre Ocala development aptly named Via Paradisus (Road to Paradise). The original design was conceived and crafted at our facility. This forged aluminum gate is magnificent in design and appearance at 27-feet wide and 28-feet tall; each side is made up of nine-foot railing and each door weighs an astounding 850 pounds. The arch was designed to represent traditional joinery with forged acorns, leaves, copper roses and 23-karat gold-leaf garland adorning it. This gate is in memory of my son, Richard Allan Chandler II, who worked with me for 15 years. He proudly took the lead on this project from start to finish and his absence is greatly felt *(Above)*.
Photograph by Kent Weekly

metal fabrication   163

"The details speak for themselves."

~Jack Klahm

This close-up view displays this entry gate's arch joinery and all the painstakingly handcrafted details. It is amazing how ironwork changes in appearance the closer one gets to it. From every angle, it is dynamic and changing *(Facing Page Top Left).*
Photograph by Mark Baret

This is actually the front entrance to my own home. The work was all done traditionally. Each of the inlaid doors weighs 200 pounds and we metallized it—which is an additional process we routinely provide for outdoor pieces—to protect against rust *(Facing Page Top Right).*
Photograph by Mark Baret

This lily chandelier was inspired by the client's affinity for British-born actress Lillie Langtry, a colorful historical character. Designed to adorn a bedroom, this forged steel chandelier was "softened" by the air brushing process, which added soft color to the lilies. This chandelier is also a very good example of the diverse projects we address. One may associate our company with large-scale projects, but we also craft inside and outside lamps, chandeliers, furniture and more *(Facing Page Bottom Left).*
Photograph by Mark Baret

This lantern is approximately 52 inches tall and is handcrafted of bronze, which is a more difficult metal with which to work *(Facing Page Bottom Right).*
Photograph by Mark Baret

This exact replication of the Titanic grand staircase center rail is from my residence. I became interested in it when I learned intimate stories of the Titanic firsthand. As a metal monger with five generations actively involved in creating metalwork, I decided to showcase my vocation with the benefit of enjoying it every day as well. The wood and inlaid metal railing is crafted of forged aluminum with airbrushed gold and walnut coloring on cast pieces. We also used an airbrushed sueding technique as well for authenticity. The blissful cherub is crafted of a bronze inlay. This staircase has been featured in many magazine articles *(Right).*
Photograph by Mark Baret

MOYER MARBLE & TILE COMPANY

Jacksonville, FL

"Correctly chosen stone or tile can accomplish any design goal. Whether that goal includes making a bold statement or even an understated interior complement, stone has that flexibility."

~Pam Moyer

This privately situated Ponte Vedra Beach home is the vacation home of Don and Chris Sallee. It was important that the breathtaking view to the Atlantic Ocean be an integrated design element from this living area. With that in mind, we chose light stone elements including the 18 by 18-foot honed travertine tiled floor which reflects the natural light and continues throughout the common spaces, as well as the magnificent hand-cut travertine fireplace. You will also notice a very prominent Italian influence which the stone columns reinforce. On the right you can also see the curvature of the wet bar's Amadeus granite countertop continued from the kitchen *(Facing Page)*.

The kitchen in the Sallee home boasts a brilliant example of Amadeus granite which was expressly hand-selected in Italy for this client. This particular granite includes components of green, plum, black and white and blends harmoniously with the Tuscan theme of the kitchen. Although you cannot clearly see the backsplash, we have hand-cut six-inch by six-inch granite squares diagonally to carry the look throughout the space *(Above)*.
Photography by Daryl Bunn of Daryl Bunn Studios

"Since 1926, the Moyer family has built a reputation on quality craftsmanship and superior service. It is something we will continue to do; this is still a family-owned business and we have our lives as well as a great deal of pride invested in it."

~Greig Moyer

This is the Wirt and Margaret Beard residence in the Ortega section of Jacksonville, situated on St. John's River. Although it is a new home, Wirt had the home built precisely and beautifully to resemble a home in fitting with the historic area. The Beard's sister-in-law, Katherine (Katherine Beard Interiors, Verona, New Jersey), designed the interior of the home and had an integral role in the countertop materials. Katherine had this very unusual Silver Sea Green granite shipped from Verona, New Jersey, for us to fabricate. It was unusual in the fact that this particular granite does not normally include such striking gold tones. Because granite is naturally occurring, there was not enough of this exact shade to fabricate the wet bar, therefore Katherine chose a complementary enameled-finish lava rock. She chose light walnut travertine flooring and a backsplash of tumbled Botticino which surrounds a hand-painted ceramic tile fruit urn behind the stove *(Facing Page Top)*.

This master bath was designed to conjure a serene, clean feeling and appearance which we achieved using this Calcutta gold marble throughout the floors, bath tub and shower. We truly consider this a masterpiece because of all the painstaking, intricate cuts made to highlight the veining of the marble and the craftsmanship which went into creating the bath tub's graceful curvature. The shower can be accessed from the two separate his and her bathrooms which incorporate it as a uniting, almost artistic element. The interior of the shower demonstrates the aesthetic power of these smaller marble tiles which match the floor as well as the complementary tile border at the top *(Facing Page Bottom)*.

Here we have a vantage point which gives one a better idea of the brilliance of the fireplace in the Sallee residence. This travertine fireplace reaches 20-feet high, seven-feet wide and was hand carved in Mexico. The craftsmanship and stunning quality of this piece make it a commanding element in the room—and the obvious focal point. Yet splendid as it is, it does not compete with the ocean view, rather it enhances the desired overall effect. The fireplace was shipped to us in several pieces and assembled by our expert and experienced craftsmen *(Right)*.
Photography by Daryl Bunn of Daryl Bunn Studios

"Inspiration for design can be found anywhere. We collaborate with our clients and their builders, architects, or interior designers to arrive at a perfect, one-of-a-kind creation for them."

~John Emery

We picked up the design of this elegant entrance from the marble pattern on the entry floor. It creates quite a cohesive appearance upon entering the home, which was our focus. We arrived at the color scheme through the colors of the flooring as well as the color scheme throughout this traditional home. In our process we use the copper foil technique, which allows for finer detail. This method was made popular at the turn of the century by Tiffany & Co. *(Facing Page)*.

Creating a charming dining area while also maintaining privacy, the design for this trio of stained-glass windows was inspired by an ornate French Empire rug design. It was possible to complement the French décor throughout this Melbourne, Florida, home—even in the windows—through this design technique. The center panel was hand-painted and fired in a kiln by master craftsman Stanley Klopfenstine *(Above)*.
Photography by Bill Kilborn

"A majority of our projects involve front entries because it's the first thing guests see upon arrival and the last they see as they leave, but stained glass is appropriate anywhere our clients can dream it, from stair railing to ceiling fixtures to lamps …"

~Jerry Preston

A whimsically patterned front door mirrors the Medieval and Baroque flavor consistent throughout the Merritt Island residence. The home is filled with wonderful European furniture including large armoires and stately pieces; we feel this door serves as an important introduction to the décor. This glass was also hand-painted and fired in a kiln by master craftsman Stanley Klopfenstine *(Above)*.

In homage to their locale, our clients desired a stained glass entry that would say "Tropical Florida." We played up the rich, tropical vegetation appreciated all over our state. To maintain the integrity of our work and also abide by hurricane standards, we double glaze and mount the stained glass to the interior of the existing safety glass *(Above)*.

Here, we also designed in a "Tropical Florida" motif. Our clients specified that they wanted their front door's design to incorporate colorful birds and butterflies; this is the resulting design. This home actually won an Aurora Award for its spectacular remodel and we were proud to be part of the team that helped transform this residence into a showplace *(Facing Page)*.
Photography by Bill Kilborn

"The concept of style begins with architecture and is then completed by the design of the interior elements."

~Troy Beasley

elements of design

To say that the highly successful design firm of Beasley & Henley Interior Design began in a whirlwind would be an understatement. Of course many young entrepreneurs would invite just such a whirlwind. Fourteen years ago, Troy Beasley and Stephanie Henley began the firm. Troy, who was in the model home merchandising field, knew he had the talent and drive to bring both to another level. At Stephanie's suggestion, they began their venture together with Stephanie heading the financial and business side while Troy drove the creative side: It was the perfect match and still is.

Today the firm employs a team of 11 including four designers with Troy as principal designer. In his personal tastes, Troy leans toward the classically modern and European eclectic, with an emphasis on rich interior architecture. When designing, he always focuses on his clients' lifestyles and desires, without the confines of any rigid style. Troy quite aptly views his role as an editor of fine things.

Beasley & Henley Interior Design can be seen across Florida and the United States, in private and commercial spaces. Troy and Stephanie have even broadened its reach into the Atlanta marketplace having opened a satellite studio there in 2006.

BEASLEY & HENLEY INTERIOR DESIGN

"Sometimes the room dictates the style of the furnishings and details."

~Troy Beasley

Although this is a new house, I find that the appropriate introduction of old architectural elements, such as the barreled ceiling complete with a striking mural, mixed with new interior architectural elements such as the oversized mirror (out of view), offer an air of Old World sophistication with a modern twist. In maintaining sensibility and conservative styling, I drew the color palette from the floor's multi-colored elements and created a contrast between quiet furnishings and those multiple colors (Previous Pages).

"Quiet sophistication." This penthouse is located in a modern condominium with a "top of the world" feel including amazing views of the city, ocean, and even The Ritz Carlton hotel directly across. Upon entering the residence, one is met with a contrasting Euro-styled table, chocolate mohair wing-back chairs and walnut-stained furniture. I formed this palette of pale golden and contrasting chocolate fabrics because it represents ease of lifestyle as well as high style with soft sophistication. The intentional position of the pieces gently directs the eye toward the outside view (Right). Photography by Steven Allen Photography

"Fabric in bold color enhances a single space, making it exotic."

~Troy Beasley

The very clean elements of this modern study interior create a lot of energy. Vibrant, fun colors are projected to inspire and energize. We had fun with this design adopting the color palette from the paintings shown. Although there are different interpretations of it throughout the space, they are tied together by the palette commonality *(Above)*.

This is my own Moroccan-themed billiard room. I desired a departure from the usual billiard rooms and this exotic, playful theme was the result. I placed pieces including the Moroccan lamp and chair for authenticity. The oasis fabric walls and framed ceiling, which is meant to mimic the underside of a canopy, actually serves two purposes: It provides the unique aesthetic charm of the room and as an additional benefit, it keeps the room virtually sound-proof. The opening of the room actually leads to our family room. Art piece by Keith Beasley *(Above)*.

We recently remodeled our master bedroom (as captured in the mirror), along with our entire house. As should always be the design goal of something as intimate as a bedroom, we wanted to create an elegant and calming sanctuary. We began with pale aqua Venetian plaster walls, which set the overall tone. The hand-carved Mexican limestone, two-way fireplace can also be enjoyed in the parallel sitting room *(Facing Page)*.
Photography by Steven Allen Photography

"Interior design is about sculpting the interior, much like an artist paints a painting."

~Troy Beasley

I believe the bold use of color stimulates and excites the senses while simple shapes calm us. This painting is the main design element in this dining room, which is then supported and contrasted by simple shapes and chairs. Contrasting effects are important; I always throw in things that may be unexpected to add this needed design element *(Facing Page Top).*

I believe that color, texture, shadow and shape are the basis for all good design. I think about every element I put together and the holistic goal of their relationship. Whether you complement something smooth with something textured or something shiny with something matte—this evokes a sense in the psyche. I encourage my clients to choose a décor influenced by what moves them. Good design will appeal to every person on an emotional level. What matters most is what the homeowner feels when they walk into their family room, their dining room, their bedroom *(Facing Page Bottom Row & Above Row).*
Photography by Steven Allen Photography

"My clients have one thing in common: They lead extremely busy lives and are looking for convenience and service. We offer sound, technological solutions that allow them to maintain and run properties worldwide."

~Wayne Kahn

In designing, consulting, integrating and installing, we are at the forefront of our industry when it comes to enhancing luxury residences all over the world with the latest technology. With capabilities ranging from lighting, custom home theater and audio-video design to engineering, system programming and project management, we are adept at blending technology with our clients' lifestyles *(Facing Page)*.
Photograph by Carl J. Thome

These striking rooms are more than average home theaters—they are modern interpretations of the movie screening rooms synonymous with Hollywood in the '30s and '40s. We collaborated with the architects and interior designers on these projects to design, deliver and install equipment that fits the function desired by the client but also worked within the confines of the overall design objectives for the spaces *(Above)*.
Photograph by Laurence Taylor

"The biggest challenge in a home movie theater is to integrate all of the latest technology into the room so that while it may be the 'centerpiece' of the room's function, it isn't the visual focal point of the room. These are beautiful suites set up to support multiple functions, like playing cards, watching sporting events or hanging out with friends. These spaces become an integral part of our clients' lifestyles."

~Wayne Kahn

To build strong working relationships with our clients, we spend time working to understand each client's lifestyle. Clients are asked about their art collections, entertaining preferences, travel interests and priorities. Each client's technological savvy is measured by studying his or her existing computers, music listening equipment, type of car, etc. This information is recorded and used as the basis for a completely custom system design *(Top, Bottom & Facing Page)*.
Top & Bottom photography by LeBlanc Studios
Facing Page photograph courtesy of Advanced Audio Design

"Well-planned lighting breathes life and drama into rooms, landscapes and structures. Light can be used to sculpt spaces and create dynamic, beautifully functioning living environments."

~Wayne Kahn

As professional lighting designers, we work with the client and design team to create breathtaking lighting solutions that enhance the architect's vision of the structure and the interior designer's concept for the rooms. Once the basic lighting plan is in place, a lighting control system is designed to make living in the spaces and actually using the lighting simple *(Facing Page & Above)*.

Facing Page photograph by Laurence Taylor
Above photograph by Ron Blakeley

"Imagination will often carry us to worlds that never were, but without it, we go nowhere."

~Carl Sagan

The overall scope of services we offer is vast. We provide systems for and integrate with: security systems, lighting control, cameras, home automation, house equipment—including pool and spa as well as HVAC—distributed audio, structured wiring, phone systems, central vacuum, wireless computer access, satellite, smoke alarms, landscape lighting, gate controllers and motorized window treatments, exterior screens and shutters. Few clients realize, before hiring us, just how much "behind the scenes" infrastructure, detail and coordination occur in order to integrate multiple disciplines seamlessly into an easy-to-use, whole-home system *(Facing Page & Right)*.

Facing Page Top Left photograph by Jennifer Dean

Facing Page Top Right photograph by Ron Blakeley

Facing Page Bottom photograph courtesy of Advanced Audio Design

Right photography by Jennifer Dean

"Two trends will cycle high in our culture: cocooning, our desire to shelter ourselves from the harsh realities of our world, and fantasy adventure, our hunger for the new and unconventional."

~Faith Popcorn

We've arranged a civilization in which most crucial elements profoundly depend on science and technology *(Facing Page & Right)*.
Facing Page photograph courtesy of Advanced Audio Design
Right photograph by Laurence Taylor

"We are committed to integrating the latest technologies as concealed amenities so that the architecture and interior design can take center stage."

~ Wayne Kahn

Perhaps the most important contribution we make to projects is interfacing with and supporting the design team, which includes the architect, interior designer, builder/contractor and landscape architect. By bringing expertise relating to the integration of systems to the project, we take all of the elements in a home and assimilate them into the client's lifestyle in a way that recognizes the most current technology but makes it easy to use and understand *(Facing Page & Above)*. *Photography by Laurence Taylor*

"Luxury, timelessness and beauty are the three defining qualities across all Clive Christian products. They link the different facets which make up a truly unique design house with a passion to endure as a future British icon."

~Clive Christian

Founded in 1978, Clive Christian Home has grown from a single kitchen studio in the town of Nantwich, Cheshire to over 40 exclusive showrooms worldwide including London, Madison Avenue, New York and Naples, Florida. Creating future design classics across an entire home collection, innovative design and uncompromising quality remain at the heart of the Clive Christian philosophy. The original building is home to the Marketing & Design offices and the original showroom which still trades today *(Facing Page)*.

The Empire Flame design tableware service is an exquisite collection of fine English bone china with a raised gold and cream ground accented by rich burnished gold. China, cutlery and crystal combine the finest materials and unique Clive Christian designs. The famous signature piece is the striking Limited Edition Caviar Comport *(Above)*.
Photography courtesy of Clive Christian Home

"World-renowned for our luxury bespoke kitchen and dining room, bedroom and bathroom, study and living room, the Home collection also includes an exclusive range of occasional furniture, china and cutlery, wallpaper, fabrics and lighting to create the ultimate living environment."

~Troy Ellis

Each Clive Christian luxury fitted and freestanding furniture piece is stamped with a mark of authenticity as a signature of high quality craftsmanship and unparalleled handmade British detail, as in this soft-closing dovetailed drawer *(Above)*.

Handmade in Britain, the timeless Empire Club Chair can be custom upholstered from a selection of sumptuous velvets available in a vast array of rich colors to complement your interior design preferences *(Above)*.

Intended for an impressive table centerpiece, this stunning Empire Flame Limited Edition Caviar Comport elegantly chills and displays the delicacy, performing its function, while making a regal statement. In high demand, there is often a waiting list for this Clive Christian exclusive *(Above)*.

Glowing blue bespoke lighting creates a moonlight effect in this Alpha Warm Walnut Kitchen to evoke a feeling of hypnotic elegance. A Clive Christian design, the walnut wood is complemented by accents of platinum leaf and the island unit has polished quartz countertops. An exclusive Alpha chandelier suspends smoked quartz crystal droplets, enhancing the drama of this fantasy kitchen. Designed for ultimate flexibility, this freestanding, modular custom furniture and wall paneling is classic and timeless, yet modern and luxurious *(Facing Page)*.
Photography courtesy of Clive Christian Home

This Regency-inspired kitchen boasts interior architecture in the Classic Cream and Gold Leaf finish with gleaming hand-applied gold accents. Beyond the impressive center mantelpiece are genuine burr oak paneled walls; the oven area is flanked by capital columns for a theatrical presentation. From the Clive Christian lighting collection, an elegant crystal chandelier with pleated silk lampshades graces the room *(Above)*.

Britain's historically renowned Royal Worcester® porcelain craftsmen create the exclusive Clive Christian Empire Flame tableware collection made of fine bone china with 24-carat gold applique´ *(Facing Page Left)*.

Clive Christian has commissioned England's famed Arthur Price silversmiths to impeccably craft our pure 24-carat gold plated Empire Flame signature cutlery with a lifetime guarantee *(Facing Page Right)*.
Photography courtesy of Clive Christian Home

"Creating the classic best-dressed table in your private residence is a rare and enviable invitation to fine dining and conversation. Giving guests the ultimate experience in opulent sophistication is mastering the art of entertaining."

~Troy Ellis

"Exquisite fabrics, luxurious wall coverings and the exclusive Clive Christian paints are quintessential elements to creating an artistic backdrop for the drama of custom furnishings and interior architecture."

~ Troy Ellis

This extraordinarily romantic and opulent Classic Cream and Gold Leaf Bedroom with genuine gold leaf accents is enveloped by imported silk and epitomizes the traditional Clive Christian custom home look. The soft furnishings include the Versailles rattan bed, nightstands and desk as well as sepia silk drapery, bedclothes and wallcoverings—all from the Portrait Number One collection *(Facing Page Top)*.

The Clive Christian Master Bedroom in Honey Oak is dressed with the identical pure silk fabrics but in a deep red hue for a dramatic ambience. The "Mayfair" four-poster canopy bed is handmade and features an integrated flat-screen television with push-button technology. Notice the traditional silk-upholstered daybed nestled between custom-fitted oak armoires lined with coordinating silk panels *(Facing Page Bottom)*.

This large-scale, contemporary gourmet interior architectural design exemplifies the Clive Christian Ivory Kitchen finish with bright stainless steel fittings for a traditional feel with a minimalist, modern attitude. Added top boxes create further storage areas above the refined cabinetry. Wicker basket drawers and a built-in butcher's block work station add warmth and natural wood to the bright kitchen space *(Above)*.
Photography courtesy of Clive Christian Home

"Understand that the kitchen is truly the heart of your home, so take great care with the design and buy the very best quality that you can afford."

~Clive Christian

Ivory and chrome with an exquisite crystal chandelier forms this feminine expression of a contemporary Alpha Ivory Kitchen. Our integrated bespoke lighting system can be tailored to the individual's taste and softly highlights the streamlined cabinetry of this custom kitchen. The freestanding landscape cooking area and high-gloss white quartz countertops create a simple sophistication *(Facing Page)*.

The Classic Cream Kitchen is a Clive Christian prototype furniture design with characteristic fluted frieze detailing, ornate dentil cornices and a cook stove mantelpiece. An elegant island with sculpted iroko wood countertop contrasts the light-colored cabinetry. A pair of crystal chandeliers are from the Clive Christian lighting collection and create a formal atmosphere *(Top Right)*.

Grand-scale appeal is the first impression of the Honey Oak Antique Kitchen with burr oak inlays and Italian marble surfaces. Details abound from beveled and leaded glass windows, carved end cupboards to oak pilasters and intricate decorative frieze elements, which can be intermingled to create a custom silhouette *(Bottom Right)*.
Photography courtesy of Clive Christian Home

"It is important for furniture to enhance the architecture of the room design within the language and context of the entire space."

~Richard Geary

This redesign project was completed in a South Beach condominium for a young bachelor. It was a particularly special project as I have been working with his family for more than 20 years, first designing his room when he was 11 years old. I custom designed this chocolate brown wenge wood entertainment center to give the illusion of a built-in piece as we wanted it to be able to move with him in the future. I chose wenge wood because as a darker wood it complements the dark Italian leather chairs, custom-designed rug and décor *(Facing Page)*.
Photograph by Joe Lapeyra

These photos demonstrate how the entertainment center was designed to have the doors fully open—without sacrificing the design—or closed when not in use—to reveal functional shelving. I also designed the stainless steel handles as I do nearly all of the hardware that adorns my furniture designs. For almost 20 years, I have had close working relationships with a trusted group of subcontractors who craft my metal and cabinetry work designs. I also designed the wall-hung bar cabinet (left in the photo) with floating glass top to minimize the appearance of any "heaviness" in the room. Although we are a small interior design firm, designing soft and hard furniture, rugs and hardware makes up a great deal of our business *(Above)*.
Photograph by Joe Lapeyra

"Although I have been classically trained in design, for the past 15 years, I have chosen to work solely in the modern vernacular. It is only through a thorough understanding of all design that came before can one understand how to create new and original design."

~Richard Geary

Inspired by my clients' desire for an additional seating option in their living room, I designed this very elemental canoe bench crafted out of rosewood veneer. Placed under a window it fits within the space perfectly without obstructing the outside view. When not in use, it serves as a set-piece on which to place a beautiful vase or sculpture *(Above Left)*.
Photograph by Ed Chappell

Designed 20 years ago, this cabinet was actually more of an experimental piece I did for a circa 1928 residence featured as a Showcase house. I wanted to add a cabinet that wouldn't visually take up space, which is why I floated the cabinet using glass panels and stainless steel standoffs. The veneer of tchitola wood complemented the cypress ceilings and heart pine flooring of the room *(Above Right)*.
Photograph by Ed Chappell

This bathroom, located in the same remodeled condominium as in the first spread, ties the same door handle design from the entertainment center with the door handle of the obscured glass door here. I find furniture and room design to be more interesting when they display a dynamic interrelation. The wenge wood pedestal sink was designed to be functional as well as sleek: The front half of the base opens for extra storage. The pedestal becomes an expression of the sink of the same diameter and the circular mirror reflects and unites these concepts *(Facing Page)*.
Photograph by Joe Lapeyra

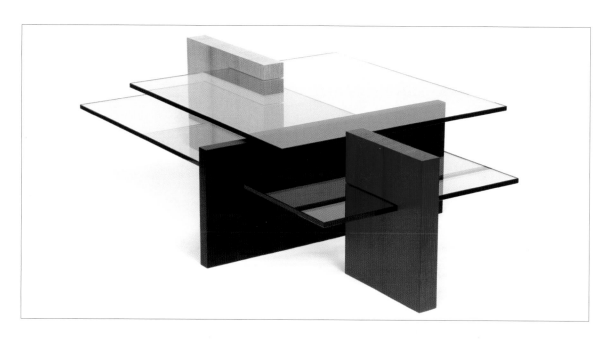

My clients wanted a spectacular coffee table to go on a rug which I also designed for them. It was inspired by the De Stijl movement of the early 20th century. This was the first design movement to abandon formal classical motifs or abstract asymmetrical form. The result is a tangible combination of transparent and colored planes which is totally abstracted *(Facing Page Top)*.
Photograph by Ed Chappell

Obviously guided by the same concepts as in the coffee table, here there are two views of a desk, both open and closed. This piece was designed on all sides as a total three-dimensional composition as well as a functional art object. Each block offers a "surprise" as it opens to reveal storage space. Then much like the outside composition, the inside displays a miniature composition of its own. I designed this personal secretary really more as a challenge to myself simply because I was inspired to do it. I reasoned that I would always be happy to have it in my own home. It lasted two weeks in my showroom before someone "had to have it" *(Facing Page Bottom)*.
Photograph by Ed Chappell

Aptly called "Ed's Bed," I designed this bed as a solution-oriented piece to solve a spatial challenge. Ed's residence was an old converted fishing cottage, and the stairway leading to the bedroom was so small that no bed was able to be moved up to it. I designed this bed so that each component could be taken in separately and assembled at its new location. It is made of steel supported wenge wood and the headboard is made of dramatic black leather. You may also notice that the side tables are part of the bed frame *(Above)*.
Photograph by Ed Chappell

"We celebrate innovation while honoring tradition, resulting in beautifully hand-crafted products that are nothing less than monumental."

~Thomas Riley

The interior of this bayfront, British Colonial estate is adorned with custom woodwork throughout. This grand room is treated with arched mahogany window surrounds and custom millwork featuring exotic burl panels on the walls and ceiling, as well as hand-scraped walnut flooring and specialty wall finishes *(Facing Page)*.
Photograph by Kim Sargent

The homeowners' request for a combination of Addison Mizner's Spanish Colonial style with a jolt of Old Cuba inspired the design for the massive ceiling in this master suite. Created from solid Spanish cedar, each beam and tongue-and-groove plank was hand-distressed by master craftsmen. The walls in this master suite are also treated with wax-polished Venetian plaster *(Above)*.
Photograph by Thomas Riley Artisans' Guild

"...od is in the
...etails."

~ Mies van der Rohe

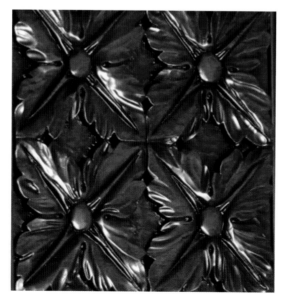

Mies van der Rohe said it best. Well-executed details, such as hand-stitched veneers, hand-carved elements, and carefully applied modern and traditional finishes are what Thomas Riley Artisans' Guild clients demand and deserve. Working closely with the project's interior designer, architect and builder, they carefully ensure that no detail is overlooked *(Top, Center & Bottom)*.
Top & Bottom photography by Thomas Riley Artisans' Guild
Center photograph by Rose Thompson

Thomas Riley Artisans' Guild is capable of executing an entire interior project or a one-of-a-kind furniture masterpiece, modern or traditional. In this grand hallway custom millwork, wall finishes and flooring have been flawlessly integrated with the inspired direction of the interior designer *(Facing Page)*.
Photograph by Kim Sargent

"A shoulder-to-shoulder work ethic and our culture of love and kindness foster a passion amongst each of us to constantly provide 'white glove' customer care—before, during and after a project."

~Matthew Riley

This Miami Beach penthouse entertainment room brings a nautical approach to an Art Deco design. The walls are fully paneled with quarter sawn, fiddle back anigre with an inlaid wave of mahogany above wainscoting with brass fittings and inlaid Yin and Yang symbols. The bar area features a custom radius front with a porthole and cantilevering shelves with glass insets in the back (Facing Page).
Photograph by Dan Forer

Thousands of hours were passionately invested in the creation of this pair of extravagant closets, leaving little to be desired. Hers, crafted from select cherry and Madrone burl, features intricate hand carving, gold-plated ormolu, and marquetry of wood and Mother of Pearl. This functional space also has an abundance of custom amenities such as individual tip-out sunglass cubbies, velvet-lined drawers, a motorized shelving system for over 400 pairs of shoes, and motion sensitive doors that open with the wave of a hand. His dressing room is a Biedermeier-inspired space that features cherry door frames and trim, olive ash burl and yew wood veneered panels and ebonized mahogany mouldings and pilasters. The custom, gold-plated knobs are inset with semiprecious stones acting as jewelry for the cabinets. Dressing in such stunning luxury, one would be hard-pressed to leave this closet (Above).
Photography by C J Walker

ARTISAN INC.

Altamonte Springs, FL

"One of my favorite things is the research before a project; keeping ideas fresh and on the creative forefront."

~Sarah E. Pelfrey

This project was commissioned by a custom builder who was constructing a very high-end spec home. Originally we intended only to address the highly decorative panel ceiling in the formal living room; however, the positive feedback was so great we continued the look throughout the moulding details in all the formal areas of the home including this view of the dining room. I drew my inspiration from the stately architectural masterworks of *McKim, Mead & White*, particularly the formal dining room of The University Club in New York *(Facing Page)*.

This is looking directly up to the underneath side of a groin or cross vault at the main entrance of a Neo-Classical Italian villa. The concept, along with the use of color, was a blending of two 15th-century ceiling frescoes found in Italy. Then, for a more personalized and custom look, the center design is one of a completely random freehand *(Above)*.

Photography by Harvey Smith of Harvey Smith Photography

"I love to artistically push the limits of Venetian plaster; then when I wax it, to see the color behind a color."

~Sarah E. Pelfrey

Decorative wood beams have made a huge resurgence in custom homes today. They range from a simple stain with the slightest hand-painted details to a very complex grouping and layering of designs, colors and aging techniques; here, the look is more graphic with clean lines. I was also able to include a few other faux painting techniques such as a faux wood grain along the upper frieze, crackle and a subtle aging to complete these one-of-a-kind beams *(Facing Page Top Left)*.

This is a great example of the versatility Venetian plaster has. Although most people may equate it with an Old World look or feel, it doesn't necessarily have to be. These walls are a very modern adaptation of this timeless technique. By combining the two blues with a vertical hand-trawled movement and a nice high polish, I was able to create a unique atmosphere for the homeowner *(Facing Page Bottom Left)*.

This 10-foot-tall frescoed orange tree was customized for the homeowners and holds special meaning to them, as they come from a citrus family. It provided a nice backdrop for their religious artifacts and entrance into their master suite *(Facing Page Right)*.

These walls were created by the notion of the homeowners walking into their own "jewelry box." It is over 1,000 square feet of silver leaf walls with an overlying damask pattern. Another interesting quality of these walls is that as you move to the side of a wall, the pattern visually fades away and the squares of the silver leaf become the prominent feature until you return to looking directly at the wall again. Top this with a free hand-painted design around the chandelier for an all around well-balanced work of art *(Right)*.

Photography by Harvey Smith of Harvey Smith Photography

C.W. SMITH IMPORTED ANTIQUES

Naples, FL

"The secret to collecting antiques is to buy what speaks to you. Even if the investment and appreciation numbers look very good, consider them secondary to the purchase ... trust your instincts!"

~Wade Smith

A 19th-century Chinese low-table supports two seventh-century Tang Dynasty pottery horses and is positioned in front of a 19th-century British Colonial mahogany linen press. In the C. W. Smith Galleries, one can observe a harmonious and unique mix of different periods and styles; all accomplished with artistic sensibility. Also, interior design solutions are much easier when the stylistic features of diverse antique furniture pieces are linear and simple in concept. For instance, this allows a large, square-corner, red-painted Chinese cabinet to blend comfortably with other design elements. This simplicity of design is one reason C. W. Smith prefers to focus on Northern Chinese areas, such as Shanxi Province, for antique furniture sources *(Facing Page)*.

A sixth-century Eastern Wei Dynasty ox and cart (left) and an early Tang Dynasty reclining camel (right)—aside from being highly desirable and collectible—offer elegant accessory solutions around which to build a room. These objects bring interesting shapes and textures as well as a pedigree supported by research and authentication testing *(Above)*.
Photography by Brynn Bruijn

"In addition to an immediate attraction, understanding and knowing about your antique purchase adds immeasurably to the satisfaction of ownership. While you don't have to be an expert, if the item you purchase doesn't create a desire to read and find out more about it, then you've only scratched the surface. To assist our customers, we make our own research available on each item."

~Carol Smith

A Ming Dynasty carved wooden Buddha sits atop a China Trade, campaign secretary made of camphor wood. China Trade and Colonial pieces are interesting in that they incorporate classic European pattern book styles with the exotic woods used in their construction. Facing the secretary is a 19th-century, square-back, bamboo chair and, on the wall, a photograph of a Tibetan monastery wall mural *(Facing Page Left)*.

A pottery figure of a Han Dynasty horse is shown on a Chinese burgundy lacquered low-cabinet in front of a colorful ancestor painting. Again, the simplicity of line (design) is the most arresting feature of this combination of antiques *(Facing Page Right)*.

Shown on this page, a large red-painted cabinet oversees a variety of British, Dutch and Portuguese Colonial pieces as well as other Tibetan and Chinese items. In both our gallery locations, we are known as the premier source for not only authentic antiquities but for design solutions utilizing our pieces. The keys to our success are in the personal acquisition of each piece in the country of origin, the offering of all items at competitive prices, insistence on thorough research and documentation and ongoing customer education *(Right)*.

Photography by Brynn Bruijn

"Most important to a home theater's success is the acoustical material. Emphasis should be placed on the highest-quality sound absorbing, reflecting and diffusing panels."

~Fred Akers

This dramatic red home theater was designed for hotelier J.W. Marriott in Bethesda, Maryland. Interestingly, we converted a rarely used indoor basement pool into this theater. An avid vintage car collector, especially of Ferraris, Bill wanted the color of the theater interior to specifically match "Ferrari Red" as seen throughout the interior from the walls to the leather seating. Further personalizing the homeowners' theater, we also incorporated a coveted collection of Hummel figurines on the glass entrance and rear walls of the theater *(Facing Page)*.

Because we are based out of Florida, yet create theater systems all over the world, we have created pre-designed theater packages and guide our clients on the logistics of lighting and sound systems. For instance, this theater incorporates a fiber optic ceiling which mimics star patterns. There are infinite options when designing a theater to make it unique to the homeowner *(Above)*.
Photography by Kenneth M. Wyner

"Offering the flexibility of a pre-designed system is the most cost-effective way for us to incorporate a theater into your home. With many packages and options to choose from, there is a concept to fit your budget and home."

~Tim Lavey

This Isleworth, Florida, vintage-themed theater combined owner Bob Noble's favorite hues and tastes. Bob wanted a classic interior of cool blues, silver and black lacquer. Also created in the homeowners' basement, there was an abundance of space in which to add authentically matched touches such as the "Refreshments" counter. The theater functions well for those who wish to relax and enjoy the show or those who want to take in the show while also munching on more than a just a snack *(Above & Facing Page)*.
Photography by Craig Zetena, Zinc Marketing

"I encourage people to only buy artwork they love. Don't let outside opinions dictate what you purchase; the art that fills your home and work environments should capture your imagination and inspire you daily."

~Shannon Basso

This is a mixed media abstract by Mactruque, a young artist from Jacksonville. I appreciate his originality, the way he uses layers of paint to create depth and movement. He is not afraid to experiment with different mediums and techniques, and this spontaneity makes his work brilliant *(Facing Page).*
Photograph courtesy of Gallery 17·92

Relatively new to our gallery, this landscape painting is by John Beard. Our clients simply fall in love with his work and the feelings it invokes. Here, he has so elegantly captured the nuances of the country landscape using a rich, multicolored palette *(Above).*
Photograph courtesy of Gallery 17·92

"Much of our attention is focused on framing—everything from children's artwork to Dali. We strongly believe in the importance of investing in good framing and we offer the highest quality conservation products available. It's simple: Proper framing will make your artwork shine."

~Shannon Basso

As you see in this painting, the artist, Enrique Mora, is often inspired by the female form. Mora uses vibrant tones to convey her strength and vitality, yet there is also a softness present. His contemporary paintings are full of color and passion, indicative of his Puerto Rican roots. I always encourage clients to keep an open mind when choosing art. Although a home may be traditional, a painting like this one is very appropriate when placed correctly. If they like the painting but are still unsure whether it will work with their décor, we offer complimentary consultation services to help them make a confident decision *(Top)*.
Photograph courtesy of Gallery 17·92

This painting is also by Mactruque. Again, you can see his exploration of his environment with color and layering, resulting in bold, intuitive works of art *(Bottom)*.
Photograph courtesy of Gallery 17·92

This incredible sculpture is by Jim Casey, a local artist who is noticeably inspired by his environment. "I grew up in the country in Central Florida, helping my paternal grandmother work on her cattle ranch. I believe the rugged Florida landscape and the architecture of the workings of the ranch have indelibly etched in my mind the rudimentary outlines of the images that have become my work." Casey is a true artist whose work is ever evolving to reflect the world around him. His pieces are sometimes designed with found objects, which he transforms into living, breathing works of art. This piece is crafted of copper wire, wood, canvas, twine and the wheels were ingeniously fashioned from a garden hose, indicating the artist's desire for authenticity and originality. Even more so than in this photo, in person, you grasp the deep passion with which each sculpture is created *(Facing Page)*.
Photograph by Everett and Soule

GULF SOUTH KITCHEN DESIGN

Fort Walton Beach, FL

"While our kitchens reflect our clients' lifestyles, tastes and design wishes, they must also be functional for that particular family dynamic."

~Richard Nivens

Inspired by an English kitchen, our client expressed her desire to adopt a similar look. We used Provence Crème paint with a fruitwood glaze to create this warm, yellow tone. Timeless cabinetry design is essential; you never want to date your kitchen. This style and color choice of the cabinetry then influenced the accompanying elements such as the golden-toned granite countertop and the gold sink fixture (Facing Page).

Shown from two vantage points—one looking outside through a bar area and another taken from the interior—this galley-style kitchen incorporates interesting light and dark contrast for a bygone-era appearance. Maintained as a vacation house, the owners wanted the kitchen to be light and bright to reflect its beach atmosphere, yet sophisticated to reflect their world travels. The dark cabinets are Black with an Old World, or "rub-through" finish; for the light cabinets we used Old World finish in Dover White with a Van Dyke Brown glaze (Above). *Photography by Keli Ann Nivens*

We used a very unique color palette in this kitchen. Because this is a vacation home on the beach, the Gulf of Mexico played a role in the home's design scheme. The blue of the cabinetry was influenced by the homeowner's appreciation of the emerald-colored waters of the Gulf, the color pattern of a beloved English china set, as well as a photo she saw in a magazine. With her direction, we formulated this distinctive color, which is Wythe Blue with a Van Dyke Brown glaze. The stained and glazed alder wood island complements the blue hue as does the matching alder wood trim detail outlining the cabinetry *(Above Left)*.

In keeping with the light, relaxing atmosphere of something as intimate as a bathroom retreat, we kept the shade of the vanity off white with a glazed finish. We are seeing an increased demand for an "Old Florida" look in our bathrooms as well as the wish for pedestal-style vanities. We encourage our homeowners to really use their imagination and let us know what they envision for their homes. Because all of our cabinetry is designed by us and created in our on-site facility, we can deliver most anything they can dream *(Above Right)*.

This expansive 450-square-foot kitchen was actually a remodel project and a thoroughly enjoyable one with which to be involved. It was designed for an active, young family who also enjoys entertaining, therefore we designed the cooking triangle and counter space around those principles. We are also finding our clients are starting to entertain more at home and even desire two cooking triangles to accommodate a two-cook kitchen. The cherry-stained and glazed cabinets hold a number of great appliances including a hibachi grill. The renovation even extended to the garage leading off of the kitchen, which we finished out with storage cabinets and shelving, essentially converting into a 150-square-foot pantry and mud room. It was a brilliant use of space and works well for the family's needs *(Facing Page)*.
Photography by Keli Ann Nivens

"As a Certified Kitchen Designer, I not only accommodate cabinetry needs, I design the entire kitchen around personal desires and strategic placement of appliances to create a total look with unity of design."

~Richard Nivens

MICHAEL SCHMIDT CUSTOM INTERIORS

Naples, FL

"Completing the interior of a home is such a team effort involving craftsmen, contractors and designers. None of us want to walk out the door until our client is satisfied."

~Michael Schmidt

In this magnificent family room, the interior designer's vision was to create grand elegance while maintaining an intimate, warm atmosphere. Designed to be a gathering place for good conversation and relaxation, seating areas are strategically placed throughout the large space. We were commissioned to build, install and upholster the benches seen in the center. We were quite pleased with the way in which the hue and richness of the fabric captured the tone of the room, carrying it from the ornate ceiling to the floor (Facing Page).

The commanding presence of this bed is perfect for this expansive master bedroom. This is a great example of how the experienced designer's vision was transformed into a reality by the efforts of a very accommodating contractor who helped engineer how the bed would be supported from the ceiling. Before production began, we made a precise template for the bed, eliminating the possibility of costly error. We made the velvet canopy in our workroom and applied it to the bed treatment on-site. I am fortunate to have such a dedicated team to support and assist me; we were all in force to complete this installation together. While on-site, we made the decisions of how it should hang in context to the room's feeling and décor (Above).
Photography by Doug Thompson Photographer

"We value the collaborative process with interior designers. They have the vision we bring to life."

~Michael Schmidt

Created for a child's nursery, this highly engineered ceiling includes fiber-optically lit stars. We added sheer fabric to the ceiling light forming a cloud which further created the ethereal effect of a starry sky. We used three different layers of fabric—white, blue and white again—to diffuse the light source and bring out the realistic blend of the light bluish color of a cloud *(Facing Page)*.
Photograph by Brynn Bruijn

In this living room, we completed the window treatment, which combined high-tech function with the timeless beauty of elegantly designed materials. The curved window was motorized and included a 20-foot-wide cornice board, which we fashioned on site and installed at a height of 24 feet. We then added the imported, hand-woven silk sheers which were sewn in the workroom using 11 half-yard pieces *(Above Left)*.
Photograph by Everett & Soule

We were very proud to be chosen to implement this project for the International Design Center located in Estero. This upholstered archway creates the first impression greeting members and visitors entering the facility. We custom fit and padded each of the sueded leather panels to the underside of the arch. The light beige color fit in perfectly with the clean décor throughout the space. It was a welcome opportunity for us, providing a little bit of a challenge, along with a nice amount of exposure for our company as well *(Above Right)*.
Photograph by Brynn Bruijn

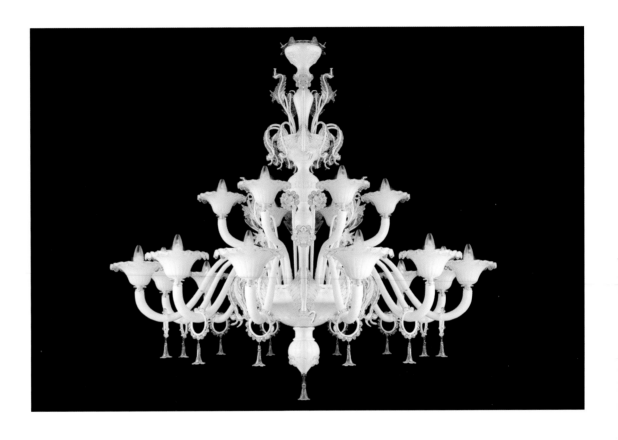

"I'm inspired by the notion of timelessness. Handcrafted treasures like Murano glass appreciate in value and are sure to become family heirlooms."

~ Marina Montmorency

On Murano, one of Venice's islands, the tradition of glassblowing dates back a thousand years. This translucent chandelier with light plum accents is leafed in 24-karat gold. It was made by Andromeda, a family-owned house that specializes in extremely high-end lighting pieces *(Facing Page)*. *Photograph courtesy of Andromeda*

It takes a master artisan to craft a chandelier as beautiful as this one. Next to the fiery furnaces, a bench is reserved for the master, who is assisted by many apprentices. This piece came from the studio of La Murrina, arguably the world's largest distributor *(Above)*. *Photograph courtesy of La Murrina*

"Nothing is more breathtaking than an elaborately hand-crafted, old-fashioned Murano glass chandelier as the centerpiece of a simple, modern room."

~ Marina Montmorency

This exquisite, swan-like chandelier by Fornasier boasts individual strands of gold glass that direction attention upward. It's a great example of how a classically flavored piece can be blended into a modern setting *(Above)*.
Photograph courtesy of Fornasier

Lighting fixtures are an amazing way to introduce color. This contemporary, amber-tinted piece by artist and maker Giovanni Cenedese was designed to emulate the shape and glow of the sun *(Above)*.
Photography courtesy of Cenedese

A more whimsical design, the orange chandelier has thin threads of glass interspersed between large tubular pieces. Custom Murano glass is a great way to turn an ordinary room into something really special *(Above)*.
Photograph courtesy of Andromeda

Lively, fettuccine-like strands intertwine to form spectacular lighting displays. This forward-thinking design was created with the same tools and techniques that have been used since the earliest days of glassmaking. Because scale is so important to consider when selecting a lighting fixture, such pieces can be modestly sized or as large in diameter as four or five feet. Larger masterpieces are sometimes personally transported and assembled onsite by the artisans *(Facing Page)*.
Photography courtesy of Andromeda

O'GUIN DECORATIVE ARTS, LLC

Naples, FL

"We are simply the artisans
who help get our clients to
their design vision."

~Cory O'Guin

Using Old World techniques and internationally recognized imported Italian materials, we developed this smooth Venetian plaster finish to complement the fabrics and other surfaces in the room. The designer wanted "the color of warm sand at sunset" as a backdrop to the client's collection of stunning art and sculptural pieces. As the light changes throughout the day, subtle variations in the appearance of the smooth, reflective surface add a quiet drama to the scene. The ceiling element is a combination of richly textured, handmade, metallic wallpaper and a coordinating finish applied to the crown moulding *(Facing Page)*.

This display niche appears in the same living area and better shows the level of detail of the wall finish. The contrast between the Dalí sculpture and the smooth wall surface makes an extraordinary statement *(Above)*.
Photography by Brynn Bruijn

"We love to work with beautiful materials. Our processes can be the star of the show, but many times they play a supporting role, quietly contributing to the overall production."

~Christopher O'Guin

Many artisans, including decorative painters, a themed artist and a trompe l'oeil muralist, labored together to make this a truly spectacular entry colonnade. An interesting element was the plaster column shafts. The interior designers described their goals for the appearance of the columns and after extensive research, we found that replicating a polished Iranian travertine stone would realize their vision of color and pattern. The marbleizing, a traditional decorative art form, required five artisans and 12 layers of hand-applied veining, glazes and clear varnishes to complete this masterpiece *(Facing Page Left)*.
Photograph by Taylor Architectural Photography

Here, we again collaborated with an interior designer who provided us with the aesthetic she envisioned for the room. We composed and installed original plaster textures that would complement the other design elements *(Facing Page Right)*.
Photograph by Taylor Architectural Photography

This close-up shot highlights the movement and depth of a custom yellow coloration that appears in an Italian furniture showroom. The designer desired a smooth, contemporary look with true Venetian plaster, of course. Classic "Stucco Veneziano" plaster treatments are very versatile; depending on the surrounding influences, they can look modern and sleek or traditionally "Old World." The smooth, waxed finish of this plaster perfectly complements the slick lacquer finish of the furniture piece *(Right)*.
Photograph by Brynn Bruijn

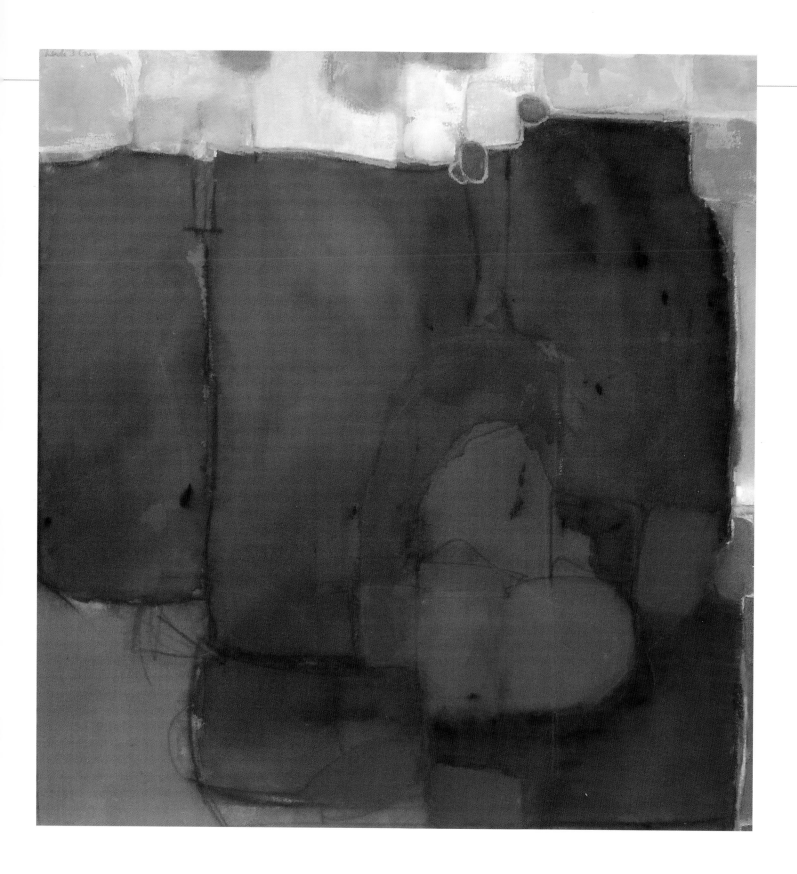

"One has seen this perfect tension before, usually in museums that house collections from antiquity. Pearson's sculptures do not borrow stylistically from anyone. All of his works have a common thread of reserve, grace and depth—qualities that have grown increasingly rare in recent times."

~Rick Moore

This abstract *Xanadu Nights* is by renowned artist Linda J. Ging. Our gallery is very fortunate to be the largest dealer of her work in the country. It has been said that Linda's paintings "are rich in color and space, evocative, at the same time, of the landscape, the elements and her internal landscape." *(Facing Page).*
Photograph by Tracy Kurtenbach

Both of these contemporary sculptures are by David Pearson. *Morning Prayer (Left)* and *Angelic Voices (Right)* are embodiments of introspection and meditative calm. A perfect artistic addition for a home's interior or added to an exterior landscape *(Above).*
Photography by Addison Doty

"Feel comfortable mixing an abstract Linda Ging painting with the other extreme of an Impressionistic Henrietta Milan— Monet feeling."

~Rick Moore

Henrietta Milan's *Monet's Love of Nature (Right)* and *Blue Treasures (Left)*. Within her original pieces, reflective of the beauty found only in nature, this artist reveres the work of old Impressionist masters such as Monet and Renoir. Milan is considered by collectors throughout the United States and Europe as one of America's most capable, contemporary American impressionist artists *(Above)*.
Photography by Tracy Kurtenbach

These rich, vivacious paintings by Lisa Linch include *All the Times You Stood by Me (Bottom)* and *Morning in May (Top)*. Much like all of her work, these whimsical paintings evoke a delightful and warm response from all who view them. Either of these paintings will create an amazing "pop" in the homes of those who are not afraid of color *(Facing Page)*.
Photography by Tracy Kurtenbach

"My first impression of the site is always something I pause to reflect upon ... design needs to respond and work with the site, beginning with the placement of the home on the property."

~Susan Hall

living the elements

chapter five

F ounder Susan Hall has been successfully pursuing her landscape dreams and those of her clients for over 20 years. Having earned her degree, this Midwest girl soon found herself in culturally diverse Florida. Fortunate to have received wonderful guidance under mentor Ted Baker, Susan opened her own firm in 1984 and operated independently until she was joined by the talents of Deena R. Bell in 1996 and Lewis Aqüí in 2002.

Best known for high-end residential design work on Florida's East Coast, the Florida Keys and in the Caribbean Islands, clients seek Hall Bell Aqüí, Inc. at blueprint stage for new construction and at all stages for restoration work. The team enjoys the collaborative efforts with architect, interior designer and client to reach the most stunning and encompassing design for the site, structure and lifestyle needs of the client.

Susan, Deena and Lewis are proud that their efforts add tremendous value to each of their clients' homes and most importantly, that each job adheres to their careful consideration of preservation for the future of Florida's environment.

HALL BELL AQÜÍ, INC.

" ... you do not need a jungle to have an accomplished landscape design ... simplicity can also be joyful and fulfilling ... As Designers, our senses of perception, observation, sensitivity and creativity are always present."

~Lewis E. Aqüí

A delightful project located in Coconut Grove on Biscayne Bay. The owner is a successful businessman with exquisite taste and it was essential that the interior and exterior of the home echo his lifestyle. The pool area achieves a very dramatic, sophisticated feel made slightly masculine with the combination of Jerusalem stone and dark wood. The deck-edge pool beautifully complements with serene elegance (*Previous Pages*).

Baja Modern best describes this symbiotic collaboration between interior designer, architect and landscape architect. This home and detached Palapa (Grass House) was designed by Altman Architects. The vibrant color selections were developed by interior designer Dennis Jenkins. The outdoor living area and pool were designed for a young, active family who would be using it often for recreation and informal entertaining. Tumbled Turkish travertine was selected as a comfortable exterior paving material for the terrace area, remaining cool in the hot Florida sun. The addition of the "firefly" flush-to-deck water features add whimsy and fun to the design (*Right*).
Photography by Lewis Aqüí

Ficus repens on the risers soften the steps that lead to the master bedroom terrace *(Top)*.

Custom-made "Thatch Garden Lights" are placed strategically throughout this Isla Morada property *(Bottom)*.

A Serpentine planter wall with a water feature gracefully enhances the organic shape of this pool *(Facing Page)*.
Photography by Lewis Aqüí

"Quality of design and workmanship leave a lasting impression on all who enjoy the garden or space in the years to follow …"

~Susan Hall

"The catalyst behind every job that I do is the possibility of creating fresh and inspiring design work that is peaceful, invigorating, bold, and subdued all at the same time."

~Deena Bell

This glass-tiled water feature enhances the central courtyard space connecting the main house to the guest quarters of this Mediterranean-style home (Above).

The existing pool was remodeled to create an inviting private paradise surrounded by lush and tropical landscape. A waterfall serves as the focal point for the pool (Above).

A spacious loggia connects the raised pool terrace to the main house. Mosaic detailed risers on courtyard steps add a vivid backdrop to the tropical foliage. Impressive custom mosaic columns transform this outdoor space into a luxurious colorful oasis (Facing Page Bottom Row).

Arrival from a long approach to a 10-acre estate home nestled on the picturesque banks of the Indian River Inter-coastal waterway (Above).

In keeping with the distinction of this 1930s' Mediterranean Revival home set forth by the original builder, Miami Beach developing legend Carl Fisher, the current owners have made it their passion to restore the home to its original grandeur inside and out. The historic significance, scale and intimacy of this home played an important role in all the stages of restoration. The formality and simplicity of the courtyard were maintained using lush and tropical foliage with a touch of delicate fragrance. The Moorish fountain with beautiful tile mosaic continues the refined details found throughout the house. The swimming pool beyond features a hand-painted mosaic by well-known artist Sergio Furnari (Facing Page Top).
Photography by Lewis Aqüí

"Uncommon luxury in outdoor living
has become our signature."

~Ryan Hughes

This sophisticated custom-designed fire pit and enchanting fire bowl warms up the poolside at evening, where homeowners can bask in the final glow of an unforgettable day. The outdoor space becomes an extension of the home's beautiful architecture *(Facing Page)*.

A triple waterfall feature is enhanced by colorful lighting to create a one-of-a-kind outdoor cooking area, a place to entertain like never before. The covered architectural structure with graceful columns allows for use rain or shine *(Above)*.
Photography courtesy of Joe Traina, Base Ten Designs

"A pool should do more than reflect the warmth of the sun. It should capture the essence of true luxurious outdoor living."

~Ryan Hughes

Handcrafted stonework and attention to detail make this refreshing lagoon-style spa the idyllic personal retreat *(Top)*.

The perfect exotic blend of imported marble and natural stone with swaying palms and flower gardens highlights this elegant, resort-inspired pool and spa *(Center)*.

The sound of trickling water is undeniably alluring, especially from a 14th-century European-style tiered fountain showcased in this charming Mediterranean courtyard *(Bottom)*.

This dramatic lighting scheme creates a special illuminated ambience for year-round outdoor entertaining—the life of ultimate leisure reflected in the serene swimming pool at dusk *(Facing Page)*.
Photography courtesy of Joe Traina, Base Ten Designs

"Welcome to a place where life is celebrated, moments are remembered, and the hurried days are soon forgotten."

~Ryan Hughes

Weaving a homeowner's style, taste and personality into a tapestry of water, stone and landscaping becomes a very individual statement with secluded privacy as well. Reminiscent of a plush resort, this backyard seduces invited neighbors and guests *(Facing Page)*.

This custom swimming pool and spa design withstands the tests of both taste and time—a welcome tropical paradise built with minimal maintenance in mind to endure for many years under Florida's sunny skies *(Above)*.

Dual fire bowls decoratively flank the infinity-edge pool, adding a radiant glow at twilight while creating a very relaxing atmosphere. The mood seamlessly transforms from day to night with an intimate and romantic feeling *(Above)*.
Photography courtesy of Joe Traina, Base Ten Designs

"Finally. Resort-style living without any reservations."

~Ryan Hughes

Stunningly bold stonework surrounds the private spa's refreshing crystal-blue waterfalls—inspired by a life well lived. Perfectly sited amidst lush vegetation, the natural design integrates into the environment for Zen-like appeal *(Above)*.

Each commissioned residential project is designed to create an extraordinary outdoor lifestyle worthy of you and your dreams. The turquoise color of the sea is echoed in the placid pool waters to provide a peaceful place to rejuvenate *(Above)*.

Handcrafted tiles, imported marble and natural stone from around the world are artistically composed to reflect the residents' sense of style and unique personality. The palm-enclosed pool and deck areas become a luxurious "island" getaway *(Facing Page)*. *Photography courtesy of Joe Traina, Base Ten Designs*

"Sometimes less is more: We like to keep our designs simple and elegant."

~Adam Alstott

The perfect complement to the luxurious Mediterranean house it sits behind, this expansive pool—16 feet by 32 feet in area—is an extension of the outdoor living space, providing residents and guests, alike, a peaceful retreat. The homeowners can easily access the pool deck from the retractable-screened porch, where they can dine by the fire in the colder months with unencumbered views to the outdoors. Both book lovers, they find the quiet haven a perfect spot to float with the latest bestseller (*Facing Page*).

Designed and constructed while the house was being built, this pool meanders under the covered bridge, spilling into the spa with its central fountain. The walled patio affords residents and guests—the red door at the top of the stairs leads to the guest quarters—privacy to enjoy the warmth and comfort the spa and outdoor fireplace provides. The confined space made it necessary to hand-dig much of the pool, yet the end result is a resort-like waterway that uniquely interacts with the home (*Above*).
Photography by Everett & Soule

"It takes a team to create the perfect water retreat. We work closely with builders, landscape architects and interior designers to conceive the best possible pool and spa designs."

~Adam Alstott

Beneath the cabana, the spa spills out around the columns and into the pool, which is simultaneously fed by the lazy river above. To contrast the cool of the water, we placed a fire pit in the pool itself—especially dramatic for nighttime swims. The slate tile that backs the spillover mirrors the home's elegance *(Left)*.
Photograph by Everett & Soule

"We are passionate about what we do, and it shows in the details."

~Adam Alstott

For the best aesthetic appeal, we chose travertine for the paver deck. Sixteen deck jets—eight on each side—shoot up and arch into the pool, which is easily viewed from many angles both inside and out of the house *(Facing Page Top)*.

For this courtyard-style home, we maximized a small space. The lion's head at the top of the rock wall is a fountain, pouring water into the basin below, which when full spills down the rocks into the pool. Glass and porcelain tiles adorn the pool's steps and the walls of the spa, which also features small waterfalls *(Facing Page Bottom)*.

For my own pool, I wanted to evoke the Bellagio. With a grotto beneath the hand-carved rock waterfall, five fountains in the spillway and a vanishing edge with a great view of the lake beyond, I feel like I'm on vacation in my backyard. I chose midnight blue for the pool floor—a dramatic contrast to the gold travertine coping. A spotlight on the grotto and underwater lighting in the spa add romance on warm summer evenings *(Above)*.
Photography by Everett & Soule

"We believe that people don't need to travel to exotic places to find paradise. We can help create personal havens just outside a client's home."

~Adam Alstott

Running almost the entire length of the house, this lap pool features four deck jets that shoot their streams from one edge into a bowl in the center of the other. Because the lot was shallow, we kept the pool narrow—six feet wide—to allow for the addition of a spa and an outdoor patio. Scuppers on the columns pour into the pool, adding to the ambience *(Above Left)*.

We enhanced the home's clean lines with a Japanese theme for the pool. The half-circle spa serves as an extension of the outdoor entertainment space, with bar stools in the pool in front to promote socializing. Opposite the spa, swimmers can relax on the bench behind the rain curtain, which falls from the wooden trellis above *(Above Center & Right)*.

Surrounded on three sides by walls of glass, the pool is the central focus of this very modern home. We mirrored the architecture's rectilinear theme in our design, bringing the edge of the pool right up to the house and spilling it into a spa below at its vanishing edge. Guests in the formal living room have a clear view to the lake beyond—the clients' goal *(Facing Page)*.
Photography by Everett & Soule

"We firmly believe that everyone deserves a waterfront view. No matter where you live, we can create one for you. Our company motto says it best: 'Have shovel, will travel.'"

~ Freddie Combas, "The Pondman™"

Originally densely wooded, the condominium complex was completely cleared to accommodate a network of ponds and waterfalls connected by streams. This waterfall feeds a pond 25 feet by 30 feet in size. Replete with water lilies, cattails and Japanese koi, and lit by underwater lights at night, the pond provides residents a soothing escape from the bustle of downtown Orlando. They can enjoy the rush of cascading falls and the light trickle of flowing streams as they amble along the nearly 400 feet of water features, all right outside their doors *(Facing Page)*.
Photograph by Everett & Soule

Our goal for the entry to the condominium complex was to greet residents with a feature that evokes a "wow" response. The large sheet of water pours over boulders—some weighing in at over a ton—welcoming residents as they arrive and setting the scene for the natural haven they will encounter as they wind through the complex. In the evening, upward-facing lights create ripples in the crashing water, dancing on the landscape and surrounding foliage. The effect is pure drama, as the light seems to set fire to the boulders and ferns *(Above)*.
Photograph by Everett & Soule

"All gardens remind one of a specific place. We want to learn where our clients most like to vacation and recreate that place in their backyards."

~ Freddie Combas, "The Pondman™"

We always discuss with clients the feeling they want their water gardens to convey. For this project, the clients wanted a departure from the tropical environment so prevalent in the area. Rather than palm trees and tropical flowers, we chose plants and trees evocative of a woodland setting. The foliage proved doubly advantageous to clients. It not only sets the desired mood but requires little maintenance, as overgrowth lends to the natural ambience (Above).
Photograph by Everett & Soule

Taking what had been a standard pool with a Mexican-inspired, blue-tiled fountain, we created a veritable lagoon, complete with tropical plants and rock features composed of a custom-bent rebar substructure along with concrete blended the natural habitat on the clients' Lake Butler site to the swimming pool. We wrapped the fountain and the adjacent Jacuzzi, which we also converted into a waterfall, in hand-carved concrete and installed drip irrigation to help the plants thrive on their own. As I do in all projects, I designed the environment to be as beautiful at night as during the day, lighting the falls from beneath to create dramatic shadows at dusk. The clients' home had large columns to support the roof. To prevent the columns from obstructing the view of the lagoon, we wrapped them with the same concrete material and hand-carved them to look like trees. We enjoyed designing this project as much as the clients enjoy relaxing in it today (Facing Page).
Photography by Freddie Combas, "The Pondman™"

"We live in the most advanced civilization known to man, yet we have less time for the important things in life—our health, families and loved ones. Knowing that what I do will provide a place and atmosphere that positively contributes to and could possibly change a client's life is what satisfies me the most about my work."

~ Freddie Combas, "The Pondman™"

For this client's home, we cleared an overgrown landscape to create an environment that blends the tropics with a wooded feel. Just above this pond is another that creates the tiered waterfall, which masks the filtration unit. Palms commingle with pines, and the assortment of plants creates contrasting textures and shades of green. To minimize the need for maintenance, I like to vary the greenery in my projects rather than adding color with blooming plants. We always strive to create the highest efficiency, lowest maintenance gardens possible *(Facing Page)*.
Photograph by Everett & Soule

This residential client turned his very large side yard into a private outdoor paradise for his frequent parties. At 45 feet by 55 feet across and six feet deep, the pond comes right up to the conservatory, giving guests an intimate view of the Japanese koi that swim in the glassy water. The pond's high-tech filtration system continuously circulates the same water, nearly eliminating the need for cleaning while keeping the pond crystal clear *(Above)*.
Photograph by Freddie Combas, "The Pondman™"

"We are changing the way that people think about living outdoors. Building an outdoor room is the least expensive way to add livable square footage to a home, and it encourages spending quality time with family and friends in the fresh air and sunshine."

~Evan Dorman

When integrating our furnishings into a space, it must be a natural fit. Here, we chose the casually elegant "Venice" collection to relax the formality of the gothic stone house. "Venice" is made from superior-grade molten aluminum. When cool, the parts are put together with 360-degree welds, hand-polished and finished in our exclusive Sherwin Williams Pecan *(Facing Page)*.

One of the first-ever fully upholstered outdoor chairs, the Biltmore chair—designed as homage to the legacy of George Vanderbilt and inspired by Louis XI armchairs—is both conceptually and stylistically brilliant. It is a perfect blend of Old World craftsmanship and state-of-the-art technology in an elegantly organic form. It was an honor to have photographed the Biltmore chair in the Biltmore Estate, still the largest home in America *(Above)*.
Photography courtesy of Summer Classics

"It's easy to design a trend. It takes mastery to design a classic. We strive to design a classic every time. We pay attention to classic proportions, superior quality and uncompromised comfort. Timeless designs, ageless beauty."

~Rob Robinson

Summer Classics' first-ever teak chair is part of a new category for the outdoor furniture industry called "Ocean." With no standard for quality in the residential category, in September 2006, we launched a series of new collections following the architectural standard "Florida 5," which mandates a material must withstand harsh ultraviolet and salt-spray testing for the equivalent of five years. We have integrated our NT1 nano-ceramic pre-wash, our proprietary N-dura resin wicker and our Burmese teak as some of the most durable materials, in their respective categories, that are available to the market. Shown here is our Ocean Grande lounge chair, which affords a comfortable and stylish way to enjoy the ocean. It features custom solution-dyed acrylic fabric, and each slat in the back of the chair has complex, milled curves. A tremendous amount of attention to detail makes this organic form both beautiful and durable *(Right)*.
Photograph courtesy of Summer Classics

"A great company is made with great people. Summer Classics is made up of dedicated, passionate individuals that strive to provide great design and inspiration to the market. We treat each piece of furniture like an architectural element. Summer Classics furniture is jewelry for every space; it's durable comfort that heightens the art of outdoor living."

~Bew White

This "Portofino" outdoor dining group is the complement to the deep seating shown previously. The sleek aluminum-slatted table is a durable and lighter alternative to wood without the bothersome splitting, cracking and paint flaking. The wrought-aluminum chair frames are woven with UV resistant and N-dura resin wicker over the reticulated foam seat and back, which allow water to pass right through. Finished in our Ancient Earth finish, the transitional, androgynous, timeless design of the chair allows it to work beautifully in a striking majority of settings *(Above)*.
Photography courtesy of Summer Classics

Technology allows us to create virtually any form we can think of. Stiffer forms work within the structure and ordered constraint of four walls. But when those walls are taken away, these once-lifelike forms seem staid and forced—curved lines simply feel more natural in outdoor furniture. The "Lauren" collection, made of loom-woven, N-dura resin wicker and cast aluminum, is our interpretation of a traditional Parsons design with energetic lines more appropriate for outdoors *(Top)*.

Color can quickly change the look of an outdoor room, and the absence of it can make you notice the details of the architecture. Here, the modern x-back "Villano" wrought-aluminum deep-seating group, shown in the silver Hammered Iron finish, is understated to the citrus hues of the flowers and subtle greens of the garden *(Center)*.

This oceanfront chat group features the Classic Wicker swivel glider, a new innovation in outdoor seating. The chair swivels and glides forward and back giving a feeling of effortless floating, which is intended to stimulate conversation. The soft greens and rich browns complement the sunshine reflections in the overhead leaves of this open-air room. The coffee table is made of never-rust slatted aluminum for durability and strength *(Bottom)*. *Photography courtesy of Summer Classics*

This oval dining set, from the "Tuscany" collection, is a sophisticated alternative to common sling furnishings. The dining chairs are crafted of aluminum tubing with milled bamboo details and faux leather woven strapping for a far more durable and beautiful product than traditional materials. Matching chaises in romantic groups of two naturally sit beside the pool. The rhythmically strapped resort chaises and "Maylay" dining group, shown in the same materials and finish as the "Tuscany" group, add stylish variation to the design of the space. Accessorized with hurricane lanterns, brick red accessories and towels add richness to this Tuscan setting. We feel that even in outdoor spaces, accessorizing is key to making a space come alive *(Facing Page)*.

Although this is an outdoor space, it truly feels like a cozy extension of the interior decor. We know if the furniture isn't comfortable our clients won't want to use it; it's just that simple. This "Portofino" sectional seating and daybed group is centered in between two criss-crossing arched traffic patterns, intended to create a focal vignette around the throughput fireplace in this unusually shaped outdoor den. Nesting tables beside the daybed give ample surface area and visual rhythm. The furniture is made by hand of wrought aluminum and N-dura wicker, the most UV resistant resin wicker in the industry (available only from Summer Classics). Because one should never compromise on quality, the "Portofino" collection, like all of Summer Classics aluminum frames, undergoes a state-of-the-art nano-ceramic prewash, called NT-1 which allows the paint to have a much stronger bond to the aluminum, resulting in a far more durable product to harsh weather conditions *(Above)*. *Photography courtesy of Summer Classics*

The "Romance" cast aluminum furnishings in this outdoor den have wide proportions and lush upholstery for long evenings by the fire. In outdoor furniture, excellence is extremely important because you want stylish, beautiful furniture that also holds up to the elements for years to come. The ornate design of twisting and turning vines has subtle references of a heart shape. This lovable furniture is finished in our hand-rubbed Ancient Earth *(Top)*.

The "Peninsula" four seasons wicker collection is a fresh and bold interpretation of the modernist-styled Parson chair. Having our parent company, Fireplace and Verandah, in business for 30 years, we lend knowledgeable guidance to our clients in choosing the right furniture for their outdoor space. We let our clients know that good design—anywhere and within many budgets—can change your life. The perfect complement to this space, its bold curves are not in wood, but rather durable, reinforced tubular aluminum finished in our exclusive Sherwin Williams, five-step Pecan finish. Outdoor fabrics adorn the group in glacier blues and rich chocolates, a sumptuous temptation of the senses. Sink into the cushions made with hypoallergenic foam and Dacron fill *(Center)*.

Dine by the pool in classic Southern style in the hybrid "Brookings" collection of wrought and cast aluminum. The aluminum slatted dining table is both clean looking, durable and will not fade or crack like wood. Our showroom is dynamic in that it allows our clients to touch and experience the furniture and the placement possibilities. This gives them confidence in the brand and themselves, while demonstrating how they can enjoy a romantic shopping experience at the store level. Our knowledgeable staff helps them find innovative design solutions that reflect the customers' personalities, styles and tastes *(Bottom)*.

This fabulous double chaise in our "Classic Wicker" collection overlooks the private ocean view under a Spanish moss-covered natural canopy of leaves. The French country pillows combined with the Nuevo baroque cabaret pillows bring an eclectic energy to this classic design of durable N-dura resin wicker, woven over a powder-coated, welded aluminum frame. Our interpretation of this classic design features wide arms, large proportions, bun feet, a diamond-back pattern and a more organic form *(Facing Page)*.
Photography courtesy of Summer Classics

"Use your outdoor space as an extension of your home. Make it a place that is beautiful and comfortable. Use it for a place to unwind, relax and exhale. Use this space as your own personal sanctuary. Utilize the area for how you live your everyday life, not for the once a year your in-laws come for a visit."

~Pat Jenkins

"Our lighting projects truly reflect our clients' desires—from guiding the homeowners through a softly lit garden path to announcing the majestic façade of their distinctive homes."

~Lisa Jewell

Homeowners or visitors have this beautiful, dramatic view to greet them as they are escorted back to the drive after an evening gathering. This stunning Mediterranean home has a deep drive and charming walk from the drive area to the front entry, which we wanted to highlight, and the last palm tree even guides them at the start of the drive. Uplighting lightly grazing the home and the arched windows continues the effect found at the front entry and master bedroom, both of which come to view at the turn of the corner. A few path lights were included to provide a welcoming glow along the paver walkway as well *(Facing Page)*.
Photograph by Larry Jewell

A picture shows it best: You can illuminate a majestic old oak with the right professional low-voltage fixture and, of course, the right design. A tree such as this is special and has a character all its own, found in the formation of the trunk, the spread of the canopy and the beautiful limbs reaching for the stars at night. Our clients are able to truly enjoy one of their property's most beautiful features from both the inside living area and outdoor living area. This oak is also lit under the back canopy, accomplishing an all-around view *(Above)*.
Photograph by Larry Jewell

"The proof is in the details: corrosion-proof fixtures, which are a must in Florida, and quality lamps that provide diversity for the desired effect. Superior products deliver superior results."

~Lisa Jewell

Professional low-voltage lighting illuminates the home as well as the surrounding landscape. We used elegant uplighting around the courtyard, the columns and the two-story entry. A truly striking approach welcomes guests and homeowners as they enter the drive, guided by the soft lighting on the lower foliage and smaller trees alongside it. Backlighting was essential and offers a contrast, creating a silhouette of the cypress in front of the home *(Facing Page)*.

These stately medjool date palms serve as an accent at the crown of the west lawn, which provides a beautiful view from inside the living area and outdoor living areas, as well as a background for outdoor entertaining on the west lawn *(Top)*.

These illuminated bird water features become part of the natural beauty of the design, with the river as the backdrop and the negative-edge water feature in the foreground. We used in-ground, grade-level lighting to obscure the light source. The key to giving the setting a natural look was keeping the background of this area dark, making it appear as though the birds wandered up from the shore to take a closer look *(Bottom)*.
Photography by Larry Jewell

TC WATER FEATURES, INC.

Orlando, FL

"The greatest confirmation of a successful project is accomplishing the clients' vision with added fundamentals that make it just right."

~Tony Caruso

Located in Windemere, this 6,500-square-foot family entertainment room posed a bit of a logistics and design challenge due to the architectural column design. It has a large amount of windows, and the light color palette reflects beautifully onto the indoor pool, allowing one to feel as though they are outdoors, no matter the weather. The pool encompasses LED, braided fiber optic lighting and flow returns. The pool flooring is crafted of an aqua pearl stone finish complemented by the room's travertine flooring, which has been polished to a high luster. Because a large consideration was the effect of a chlorine mixture on an enclosed area, a chlorine generator constantly sanitizes the water *(Facing Page)*.

This outdoor pool, with aesthetic deck spray and fiber optic waterfalls, takes on a decidedly Margaritaville look. The homeowners desired everything at the touch of a button and we designed every function of the pool to be achieved in just that manner. The pool and spa are fully automated with electronically controlled plumbing runs, LED lighting, heat and flow differential. The spa's flooring was inlaid with unique Art Deco tiles and the surrounding deck was designed in a gold travertine *(Above)*.

Photography by Eric Cucciaioni Photography

"Our strong point is, without a doubt, the ability to give motion to water."

~Tony Caruso

This is a closer detail view of the pool shown on the previous page. It offers one a better idea of how the cascading waterfalls and deck spray create a lovely effect *(Facing Page Left)*.

This fountain actually appears in the backyard of the home which features the indoor pool (shown on the first page). This family appreciates the beauty of water elements on their property; we created a fountain in front of their home as well. A water oasis was created in this multi-leveled waterfall. We call this the "mini Taj Mahal." At 80 feet long, 16 feet at its widest point and eight feet at its narrowest point, the fully automated fountain runs on one pump and on plumbing placed 100 feet away. It is lined with one-inch-by-one-inch glass tiles and a quartz interior finish *(Facing Page Right)*.

Found in an intimate side courtyard morning area, this pre-cast one-of-a-kind lion's mask wall fountain, with small blue wall tile, is a quietly commanding design element. When lit at night, it stirs drama and adopts a whole new tone *(Right)*.
Photography by Eric Cucciaioni Photography

publishing team

Brian G. Carabet, Publisher
John A. Shand, Publisher
Phil Reavis, Executive Publisher
Sheri Lazenby, Group Publisher

Beth Benton, Director of Design & Development
Julia Hoover, Director of Book Marketing & Distribution
Elizabeth Gionta, Specialist of Editorial Development

Michele Cunningham-Scott, Art Director
Mary Elizabeth Acree, Graphic Designer
Emily Kattan, Graphic Designer
Ben Quintanilla, Graphic Designer

Rosalie Z. Wilson, Managing Editor
Katrina Autem, Editor
Lauren Castelli, Editor
Anita M. Kasmar, Editor
Ryan Parr, Editor

Kristy Randall, Managing Production Coordinator
Laura Greenwood, Production Coordinator
Jennifer Lenhart, Production Coordinator
Jessica Garrison, Traffic Coordinator

Carol Kendall, Administrative Manager
Beverly Smith, Project Management
Carissa Jackson, Sales Support
Amanda Mathers, Sales Support

PANACHE PARTNERS, LLC
CORPORATE OFFICE
13747 Montfort Drive, Suite 100
Dallas, TX 75240
972.661.9884
www.panache.com

FLORIDA OFFICE
407.925.9488

Jonathan Parks Architect , *Page 25*

publisher's note

I hope you enjoy this amazing collection of work from artisans who will inspire you to create your very own dream home or maybe just a dream space. I love great design and I love to surround myself, my family and friends with a warm and inviting space in which to live, play, entertain and work. Who knew along the way I would learn so much about today's technology in home security or how lighting and paint can change the entire look of a room?

Thank you to all of the artisans who collaborated with me in creating this book. Thank you for sharing your passions, inspirations and love of what you do with not only me but with our readers. Thank you to Beth for your support along the way, our entire production and creative team and the photographers who bring to life these magnificent works of art. Last but not least, thank you to Beal and Jordan who continue to inspire me and support what I love to do.

All the best,

Sheri Lazenby

Sheri Lazenby
Group Publisher

resource index

Advanced Audio Design 183
  Wayne Kahn
  2400 Trade Center Way
  Naples, FL 34109
  239.596.3421
  www.Advanced-Audio.com

Amazon Metal Fabricators 151
  Don Benson
  600 Cox Road, Unit C
  Cocoa, FL 32926
  321.631.7574
  Fax: 321.631.2799
  www.amazonmetal.com

Architectural Artworks Incorporated 121
  Roland J. DesCombes
  Joan DesCombes, CKD
  268 West New England Avenue
  Winter Park, FL 32789
  407.644.1410
  www.arch-art.com

Artisan Inc. 217
  Sarah E. Pelfrey
  403 Westchester Drive
  Altamonte Springs, FL 32701
  407.925.3413

Beasley & Henley Interior Design 175
  Troy Beasley
  Stephanie Henley
  919 Orange Avenue
  Winter Park, FL 32789
  407.629.7756
  www.beasleyandhenley.com
  IB1038

Clive Christian Home 195
  Troy Ellis
  International Design Center
  10800 Corkscrew Road, Suite 101
  Estero, FL 33928
  239.949.3010
  Fax: 239.948.3857
  www.clive.com

C.W. Smith Imported Antiques 221
  Wade Smith
  Carol Smith
  1260 Third Street South
  Naples, FL 34102
  239.213.0749

  4424 Excelsior Boulevard
  Minneapolis, MN 55416
  952.922.8542
  www.cwsmithinc.com

Davis Dunn Construction, Inc. 59
  Whitney Davis
  Will Dunn
  150 Industrial Park Road, Suite 5
  Destin, FL 32541
  850.654.9152
  www.davisdunn.com

Erickson Associates 17
  Carl Erickson
  849 7th Avenue South, Suite 201
  Naples, FL 34102
  239.643.1999
  www.eaarchitecture.com

Feature Presentation 225
  Fred Akers
  Tim Lavey
  4189 L.B. McLeod Road
  Orlando, FL 32811
  407.648.2455
  www.featurepres.com

Florida Water Gardens, Inc. 277
  Freddie Combas
  1600 West Fairbanks Avenue
  Winter Park, FL 32789
  407.679.7787
  www.floridawatergardens.com

Gallery 17·92 229
  Shannon Basso
  912 South Orlando Avenue
  Winter Park, FL 32789
  407.647.1792
  www.gallery1792.com

Geary Design 205
  Richard Geary
  5353 Jaeger Road
  Naples, FL 34109
  239.594.1600
  www.gearydesign.com

Get Organized, Inc. 155
  Ben Benkiran
  4380 36th Street
  Orlando, FL 32811
  407.839.6225
  www.getorganizedinc.com

Gulf South Kitchen Design 233
  Richard Nivens, CKD
  707 Anchors Street NW
  Fort Walton Beach, FL 32548
  850.244.1522
  www.gulfsouthkitchendesign.com

Hall Bell Aqüí, Inc. 253
  Susan Hall
  Deena Bell
  Lewis Aqüí
  7520 SW 57th Avenue, Suite "G"
  Miami, FL 33143
  305.663.6077
  Fax: 305.663.6763

  4425 Crooked Mile Road
  Merritt Island, FL 32952
  321.449.0790
  Fax: 321.449.0745
  www.hallbellaqui.com

The Hill Group 67
  Toby Hill
  3880 39th Square
  Vero Beach, FL 32960
  772.567.9154
  www.thehillgroup.biz

The Hughes Group 261
  Exterior Design and Build
  Ryan M. Hughes
  1331 Gunn Highway
  Odessa, FL 33556
  813.792.9966
  Fax: 813.792.9977
  www.hughesgrouponline.com

Hyland Custom Cabinetry 159
  Chris Hylemon
  Rob Rieland
  6210 Shirley Street, Unit 102
  Naples, FL 34109
  239.598.1604
  www.hylandcustomcabinetry.com

Island Tile & Stone, Inc. 127
  Laurie Fourmont
  645 Beachland Boulevard, Suite 6
  Vero Beach, FL 32963
  772.231.3860
  www.islandtileandstone.com

Jonathan Parks Architect 25
  Jonathan Parks, AIA
  1471 5th Street
  Sarasota, FL 34236
  941.365.5721

Klahm & Sons 163
  Jack Klahm
  2151 NE Old Jacksonville Road
  Ocala, FL 34470
  352.622.6565
  www.klahmandsons.com

Michael Schmidt Custom Interiors 237
Michael Schmidt
5435 Jaeger Road, #101
Naples, FL 34109
239.254.7933

Morales Construction Company, Inc. 75
Rick Morales
6950 Phillips Highwway, Suite 15
Jacksonville, FL 32216
904.296.9559
www.moralesgroup.com

Moyer Marble & Tile Company 167
Greig, Glenn, Gary, Pam & Stephanie Moyer
11657-2 Phillips Highwway
Jacksonville, FL 32256
904.260.7573
www.moyercompany.com

Murano Glass Creations 241
Marina Montmorency
10800 Corkscrew Road, Suite 148
Estero, FL 33928
239.450.6844
Fax: 239.592.7852

Mystic Granite & Marble. 101
Darlene Spezzi
100 West Colonial Drive
Orlando, FL 32801
407.872.7717
www.mysticgranite.com

Newbury North Associates. 83
David S. Rogers
1010 Central Avenue
Naples, FL 34102
239.434.2668
www.newburynorth.com

O'Guin Decorative Arts, LLC 245
Christopher O'Guin
Cory O'Guin
5650 Yahl Street, Suite 4
Naples, FL 34109
239.434.9999
www.oguindecorativearts.com

Olde World Cabinetry 133
Nancy Braamse, CKD, CBD, Florida Licensed
Interior Designer #4041
6483 Ulmerton Road
Largo, FL 33771
727.530.9779
www.oldeworldcabinetry.com

Outdoor Lighting Perspectives®. 293
Lisa Jewell
18 South Riverside Drive, #103
Indialantic, FL 32903
321.821.2244
www.outdoorlights.com

Pellegrini Homes, Inc. 91
Linda Pellegrini
5728 Major Boulevard, Suite 176
Orlando, FL 32819
407.352.9100
www.pellegrinihomes.com

Preston Studios 171
John Emery
Jerry Preston
552 South Magnolia Avenue
Melbourne, FL 32935
321.259.0044
www.prestonstudios.com

Randall Stofft Architects 33
Randall Stofft
42 North Swinton Avenue
Delray Beach, FL 33444
561.243.0799
www.stofft.com

Richard Skinner & Associates,
P.L. ARCHITECTS 41
Richard G. Skinner III
2245 Saint Johns Avenue
Jacksonville, FL 32204
904.387.6710
Fax: 904.387.1413
www.rs-architects.com

Rick Moore Fine Art Gallery 249
4230 Gulf Shore Boulevard
Naples, FL 34103
239.434.6464
www.rickmooregallery.com

SAFE - Strategically Armored
& Fortified Environments. 139
Al V. Corbi
Los Angeles, CA 323.822.9520
Washington, D.C. 202.484.9500
www.SAFEnvironments.com

Savoie Architects, P.A. 49
Matthew C. Savoie, AIA, NCARB
Andrea J. Plunk, AIA, NCARB
6346 West County Highway, 30A
Santa Rosa Beach, FL 32459
850.622.0057
www.mcsavoie.com

Summer Classics at Fireplace & Verandah. 289
Patricia Jenkins
738 US Highway 17/92
Longwood, FL 32750
407.262.8115
www.fireplaceandverandah.com

Summer Classics, Fine Outdoor Furnishings. . . 283
Corporate Office
7000 Highway 25
Montevallo, AL 35115
For more information call toll free: 888.868.4267
www.summerclassics.com

TC Water Features, Inc. 297
Tony Caruso
Tina Caruso
12484 Lake Underhill Road
Orlando, FL 32828
407.282.4911

Thomas Riley Artisans' Guild. 211
Thomas Riley
Matthew Riley
1510 Rail Head Boulevard
Naples, FL 34110
239.591.3203
www.thomasriley.net

Tischler und Sohn 111
Corporate Headquarters
800.282.9911
Design Center of the Americas Showroom
954.920.8800
www.tischlerwindows.com

Tropical Pools & Spas. 269
Adam Alstott
587 Ruby Court
Maitland, FL 32751
407.331.5006
Fax: 407.331.3558
www.tropicalpoolsandspas.com

Wonderland Products 145
Joe Ponsler
5772 Lenox Avenue
Jacksonville, FL 32205
904.786.0144

the PANACHE portfolio

Dream Homes Series

Dream Homes of Texas
Dream Homes South Florida
Dream Homes Colorado
Dream Homes Metro New York
Dream Homes Greater Philadelphia
Dream Homes New Jersey
Dream Homes Florida
Dream Homes Southwest
Dream Homes Northern California
Dream Homes the Carolinas
Dream Homes Georgia
Dream Homes Chicago
Dream Homes San Diego & Orange County
Dream Homes Washington, D.C.
Dream Homes Deserts
Dream Homes Pacific Northwest
Dream Homes Minnesota
Dream Homes Ohio & Pennsylvania
Dream Homes California Central Coast
Dream Homes Los Angeles
Dream Homes Michigan
Dream Homes Tennessee
Dream Homes New England

City by Design Series

City by Design Dallas
City by Design Atlanta
City by Design San Francisco Bay Area
City by Design Pittsburgh
City by Design Chicago
City by Design Charlotte
City by Design Phoenix, Tucson & Albuquerque
City by Design Denver
City by Design Orlando

Spectacular Homes Series

Spectacular Homes of Texas
Spectacular Homes of Georgia
Spectacular Homes of South Florida
Spectacular Homes of Tennessee
Spectacular Homes of the Pacific Northwest
Spectacular Homes of Greater Philadelphia
Spectacular Homes of the Southwest
Spectacular Homes of Colorado
Spectacular Homes of the Carolinas
Spectacular Homes of Florida
Spectacular Homes of California
Spectacular Homes of Michigan
Spectacular Homes of the Heartland
Spectacular Homes of Chicago
Spectacular Homes of Washington, D.C.
Spectacular Homes of Ohio & Pennsylvania
Spectacular Homes of Minnesota
Spectacular Homes of New England
Spectacular Homes of New York

Spectacular Wineries

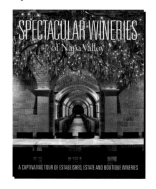

Spectacular Wineries of Napa Valley

Additional Titles

Spectacular Hotels
Spectacular Golf of Texas
Spectacular Golf of Colorado
Elite Portfolios

**Visit www.panache.com or call
972.661.9884**

PANACHE PARTNERS, LLC

Creators of Spectacular Publications for

Discerning Readers